Log Cabin Escape.

Three

"He leads me beside the still waters."

**A Christian based Novel
by
Arnold Kropp**

This is a work of fiction. Names, characters, businesses, places, events, locales, and incidents are either the products of the author's imagination or used in a fictitious manner. Any resemblance to actual persons, living or dead, or actual events is purely coincidental.

The use of the name of Jesus and all references to God are spiritually intended.

Scripture references are from the AKJV.

Log Cabin Escape Three

Author: Kropp, Arnold

ISBN:979-8-218-21643-6
E pub:

Yes, I dedicate this to all my grandsons.

To Rita, my editor, and others who've suggested changes and corrected my grammatical mishaps.

Thank you. Thank you.

LOG CABIN ESCAPE,

THREE

"He leadeth me beside the still Waters."

~ 2 ~

One

"Fran, wake up," Sam shakes her arm. "You'll be late."

"Huh? What time is it?" she answers.

"Come on, get up. I've already taken King out, and now have your tea ready."

She rolls over, covers up in the blanket, and pulls the pillow over her head. "One more time to get you up, or I'll call announcing you're sick and will not make it today." No response from Fran, except for her adjusting the pillow.

"Okay then," Sam says, taking ten loud steps to the kitchen table. He opens and closes the icebox, and sips his coffee, loudly turns the book pages. He opens the stove and blows on the embers creating sparks, shuffles his boots against the floor, sighs, coughs, drops the spoon, pushes the chair back, rises, and opens the door for King.

"Oh, you and your noisy stuff this morning," Fran mutters after throwing the blanket off and stands. "Oooh! It's cold," and she rushes past the closet and into the bathroom.

King runs toward her, barking as she closes the door. The dog barks a few more times, turns and returns to sit near Sam at the butcher block table, gets a good rubdown, and then jumps onto the couch by the fireplace.

Fran emerges from around the wall separating the living area from the closets and bathroom in her wool robe, socks, and slippers. "Oh, Sam," she loudly says. "I'm going to be late. Need your help. Warm up the car for me as I get dressed."

"On it," he replies. Sam bundles up, and opens the cabin door. King runs out ahead of Sam. He starts her car, turns on the heat, and drives it out and back from the entrance road to make a path in the fresh snow. He parks it in front of the cabin porch just as Fran comes out and carefully steps off the porch into the fresh snow viewing the snow-covered gazebo, the still waters of the lake, the tree branches bending from the new snow, and the tire tracks out to the road.

"Here it is," Sam tells her as she approaches. "Have a good day," he says, throwing his arms around her.

"You did all this already?" Fran says.

"We got another three to four inches last night. Take it slow and easy up the path. The main road is okay." He leans in to kiss her.

"Thank you so much. Sorry, but the bed was so comfortable I didn't want to get up. It'll take me a while to get used to this." Fran says as she slides into the front seat. "I'll let you know when I get there." And off she goes to the hospital in Johnsonville with King barking and jumping alongside the car.

Sitting in the rocker on the deck, Sam watches as King comes running back onto the porch next to Sam. "Well, buddy, what are we gonna do today?" Sam rubs King behind the ears and down his back. He stands and starts the walk to the barn. Sliding the barn door open, Sam sees his horse standing in its stall. He rubs behind its ears and down its neck. He fluffs the thick blanket, fills the water bucket, and tosses more hay into the corner of the stall. Sam pushes the rake to clean the stall and adds a layer of loose hay. King barks at the horse, and it rises, kicking its front legs out at King.

"Stop it, King," Sam yells. "Come, let's go warm up. Wonder will be fine."

Entering the cabin, Sam warms his coffee, fills his travel cup, pockets the list, gets the truck keys, and closes the cabin door. He opens the truck door to let King jump in to sit on the passenger seat. Starting the truck, Sam rubs his glove-covered hands together, adjusts his cap, waits a moment, and starts the drive into town. He finds a spot near the diner, rolls King's window down a bit, and strolls into the diner.

"Well," Joanna says. "Hey everyone, look who has just come in." The dozen or so folks cheer, and some come over to greet Sam. The first to greet Sam is Gene and Marjorie. Next to them are Jack and Joyce Ripper.

Gene updates Sam on the removal of the tent and the chairs. "It was a great ceremony, Sam. King, wow. That must have taken some time to train him to do all that. We'd love to have you and Francinea over to the house when you get the chance. The scouts want another camp-out."

Sam turns to Jack, "I thought you were gonna spend the winter in Florida."

"Ah," Jack replies. "We were, but my son and his wife got sick and told us not to come."

"Oh, sorry about that. Are they okay now?"

"We haven't heard from them since. They're not returning our calls. But hey, It's good to see you again."

Joanna interrupts the greetings, "Hey, y'all, let Sam relax and have a donut this morning." She leads Sam to join Pastor Thomas and his wife in a booth in the corner. "I'll get your coffee."

"Good morning, Sam," Pastor Thomas says. "Francinea back to work?"

"Yes. So, how's everything around here? I've missed it, not the snow and cold, but anyway, it's great to be home again."

"You surprised us all. So, where did you go?"

Joanna sets the coffee cup in front of Sam, along with a donut. "Anything else, Sam?"

"No, that's it. Thanks."

"It's good to have you back," Joanna says, leaving the booth.

Mary says, "Fran had indicated you'd be in the cabin for the honeymoon. Then it was discovered you had left. Sheriff Olsen told us he knew but wouldn't say more."

"Yes, we did. The next morning we drove to Denver to catch a flight to Houston. Rented a car there and went to a beach resort at Galveston."

"Thought you must have gone south noticing your tan-colored face," Thomas says. "It's good to see you, and now any other plans?"

"Haven't even thought about tomorrow. All I know is that I had been wondering if King would remember us. When Meredith brought him to the cabin yesterday evening, he jumped and just about pushed me off balance. Now, I guess it's adjusting to snowy cold weather again."

"How's Fran adjusting?" Mary asks.

"She's got a shift at the hospital today. Like we say, one day at a time, Lord."

"That offer for you to lead a weekly bible study still stands. Have you given it any thought?

"No. I really haven't. Tomorrow, I'll go see how the young rascals are doing. And, as far as a bible study, I don't know. You know me, I ramble on, and there's no telling where it might go. I don't think I could stay on a subject, and that seems, to me anyway, not what a bible study is. I have a hard time remaining on the content when reading Scripture. There's always a question that arises for me."

"What I was thinking is just concentrating on Genesis. The story of creation," Pastor Thomas says.

"Oh. While in Galveston, we got to know a couple from New York. He is a microbiologist, and his wife is a neurologist. They were there to escape the madness in New York for a few weeks. Boy, we had some interesting conversations. He was not a Christian and said the creation story was pure myth, yet he did not go along with the big bang story either. The one thing I've learned since coming here is to ask questions until the answer comes. That's how our conversations developed. Fran intently listened to Naomi, his wife, delve into our nervous system controlling all we do and are. It was great. They were very interested in my cabin life, as he also had memories of his grandfather's cabin in Maine. When they left, Richard told me he would search the creation story deeper and thanked me for opening him into a realm he had always dismissed as unscientific. I prayed for them, and he thanked me for that."

"God was working through you, Sam." Pastor Thomas says. "And now, back to us here. Please consider leading a weekly study for our folks here, who may have the same deep-down confusing thoughts about what the world teaches and the reality." He looks to his wife, "Well, Mary, we need to go. I've got some studying to do for my sermon Sunday. Thanks, Sam. We enjoyed it. See you Sunday morning." They get up and leave the diner.

Joanna comes with a refill of Sam's coffee.

"So, Joanna, what's the latest rumor? Are you being good?"

"Me, good? Ha, I'll be good when you look the other way."

"Well, God has been good to you, so be good to me and pay my bill. You could even leave me a tip for bothering you."

"I'm going to bother you right now. Take your dishes to the kitchen," Joanna replies, and her gum-chewing intensifies as she leaves to wait on another.

Sam leisurely sips the coffee, then wraps a five-dollar bill in the napkin and gets up to leave. Back in the truck, he stops at the grocery store. He gets a high five from Paul after serving Sam a sliced ham. He scans the list Fran left for him to get as he enters the check-out line. "Okay, got it all," He mumbles.

After placing the bags in the back of the pick-up, he heads to the ice plant. Gets a ten-pounder and renews his scheduled visits. He stops at his mailbox, retrieves all, and starts the short drive down the path to his cabin. Halfway there, he meets the sheriff's vehicle near the turn. The red lights come on, and the sheriff backs to the gazebo. Sam parks his truck in front of the porch.

"I heard you had returned and came for a visit, and here you are?" Sheriff Olsen tells Sam. King jumps out to greet the sheriff.

"Yeah, I had to get a few items and coffee from Joanna. Good to see you. Come on in."

Sam carries the groceries into the cabin and starts putting things away while the sheriff brings in the block of ice. He places the ice in the bottom section of the icebox. Sam pours sheriff Olsen and himself a cup of coffee. They sit in front of the fireplace as King sits on his favorite cushion beside the chair.

"So, Sam, was Galveston as I told you? The resort, the beaches. Did you get out and do some deep-sea fishing? How did Fran like it?"

"Oh, sheriff, it was wonderful, and getting away from the cold for those ten days was relieving. We had a great time. Yes, we did get out for fishing, but it was on the island's northern side. Caught some speckled Trout. Fran enjoyed the scenery. Oh, from now on, holding the rod and reel here is kids play compared to that. I fish on the lake for food, whereas the activity of fishing there was for enjoyment. Did we eat the speckled trout? No. We enjoyed the beach more than anything."

"Looks like you got a tan."

"Oh, yeah, and next was talking with other tourists from all over the country. One couple caught our attention. He is a microbiologist scientist spending most of his time peering into microscopes examining cells, atoms, exploring that unseen world. His wife is a neurologist. During an hour of dinner with them, he wanted to know more about my log cabin life. We had dinner the next day and the next. I gave him a copy of the Log Cabin Life memos I have written."

"Take any pictures?"

"Fran did. We had a great time. Thanks for introducing the idea to us and securing our reservations. So, how's it been around here? Any uprisings? The young rascals, how are they doing?"

"It's been quiet since you were not here to stir things up," The sheriff laughs.

"Okay then, I'll get things rolling again in a few days after adjusting to this snow. One morning, as Fran had gone for a massage, I was relaxing next to several palm trees by the beach. Now, don't tell Fran about this. Those beautiful young women sunbathing caught my eye. I sensed I had been transformed into an Eve-type garden. I imagined Adam falling away under those circumstances, but for an apple, a fruit he'd never tasted."

"So, did you?"

"Did I what?"

"Get together with the girls."

"Sheriff, you, the mayor, and the governor tell us of the things we must not do, and we, well, most of us obey. But when we read the commandments or hear that still voice telling us not to do something, we pretend we did not hear or understand. The fine, the cost of disobeying you all, is relatively nothing …. "

The sheriff's phone rings. He answers.

"Sorry, Sam, I've got to go."

Sam has reclined on the rocker on the porch as King runs back from running alongside the vehicle. "Shall we go for a walk?" he asks his pet.

"Woof! Woof!"

"Okay." Sam puts on his hiking boots, a warm cap, gloves, and jacket, and off they go toward the pier and left into the woods and to the stream. Periodically he bends down to grab a handful of snow and throws it in front of King. Another one hits King on the side. King stopped and shook the wet snow at Sam. They reach the stream area. Sam shakes the snow off the chair, rubs the seat, sits down, leans back, and views the snow-covered mountains. He closes his eyes. *Oh, it's beautiful.* Sam wonders. *Are there places on this planet where the forest and snowy mountains meet sandy beaches like those in Galveston? Go skiing down the slopes, stop on the sand, and then jump in the warm water. Yes, where would that be? To experience two different environments in a minute. Hmm? I suppose that's how it'll be when we die. Experience this physical earth and then heaven. Will we still have our five senses?*

King takes off running after a squirrel.

Sam pushes himself up from the comfortable chair and starts walking back to the cabin. Soon King catches up to Sam, holding a rabbit in his mouth, and drops it at Sam's feet. "Oh, now Fran's got something to fix us for dinner." Sam picks it up by the tail and continues the ten-minute walk back to the cabin. He puts the rabbit in the icebox. He gets grandma's recipe notes, finds one on how to prepare and cook a rabbit, and reads it.

"Okay. Later. Now I got a couple of hours to read.*"* After placing three logs on the fire, he comforts himself on the couch in front of the fireplace. He opens the book about Josephus and starts to read where he left off before the honeymoon. *Oh, Josephus, what a guy he was to delve into ancient history as he did. He was born in the early first century. From his beginnings, he loved literature, began to write, and eventually wrote detailed accounts of ancient history. Yeah, way back then. No typewriters, just feather tips dipped in some kind of ink. It's a shame to our modern education that his writings are not read or analyzed. Grandpa has three of his works. I thought I'd enjoy reading more, but my mind now is like Humpty Dumpty.*

Sam puts the book down and rubs behind his dog's ears, snoozing next to him. He gets up and moves into the kitchen area. Carefully places two logs in the stove. He retrieves the rabbit and starts to dress it down. He removes all the fur from the tail to the neck, grabs the thin skin layer below the neck, and pulls it to the rear. Next, he carefully removes the heart and lungs, and all entrails. Laying that aside, he pumps water into the pot and sets it on the back of the stove to warm. He adds olive oil, some sliced mushrooms, and chopped cabbage to let that warm a bit while Sam cuts the meat into pieces. Tests the water, adds a pinch of pepper and salt. And then cuts pieces of the rabbit and let them warm. He opens the door of the stove to control the heat.

"Okay," Sam tells King. "I'll let that simmer for a couple of hours. Here," he gives King a treat. "Now, whether Fran will enjoy this, I don't know. But it'll be ready to fry when she gets home."

Sam sits at the desk, inserts a piece of paper, and starts typing.

My Cabin Life 23

Here it is, the second day back from our honeymoon in Galveston, Texas. What a wonderful time we had, enjoying the sunny warm weather and the conversations with other vacationers. The resort the sheriff recommended was the best. We were on the fourteenth floor, and from our balcony, we could watch the ocean waves rumbling to the sandy beaches where youngsters were riding the waves. Many couples were relaxing on their lounges under umbrellas, some letting the sun tan their bodies. And, of course, lifeguards spaced a hundred yards apart, watching it all. What a tedious job that must be.

Wow. Never before had Angelia and I taken a vacation such as this. We could have, but the subject never came up. And now, my second wife, Francinea, and I did.

One couple caught our attention, or was it the other way around? They joined us at dinner one evening, and when he heard me say I was living in an ancient log cabin, he wanted to know more about that. He intently listened. Before leaving on this trip, I asked Judith at the library to make copies of my cabin life notes for me. So, I gave him a copy to read. The next day, he said he was fascinated with it and wanted to know more, but as an agnostic, he couldn't agree on the creation story and wondered how we could.

As a scientist, he emphasized that he's learned how cells work and evolve. He explores the inner workings of cells as seen through microscopes and how we have many of the same elements as previous humanoids, only a bit more complicated as our species evolved over millions of years.

His wife said she had been leaning toward the creation story for the last couple of years but said it's difficult, especially when everyone around you is a scientist.

I said, "Easy. Recorded in history. Revealed in nature." Then I told him of my conversion.

Yes, he listened and did not disrupt. We were scheduled to leave the next day, so I asked if he'd object to my prayer for him and his wife. I did, and he thanked me. We promised to keep in touch.

We took one more run to the beach in the morning and then the drive back to Houston for the flight to Denver. Sitting in the plane, Fran showed me the hundreds of pictures she had taken to be in our honeymoon album. A few she wants to enlarge and hang on the cabin walls.

There are certain memories one wants to keep, and this honeymoon is at the top of the list.

Thank You Lord.

He starts to re-read his notes when Fran opens the door.

"Well, hey," Sam says, getting up from the desk and rushing into her arms. "How was it?"

"Hi, honey," she replies. "You've been writing again. I'm hungry. Let's go."

"Oh, I got something warming up, but if that's what you want, sure."

"I thought I smelled something." She turns and looks at the stove and takes the few steps to look in the pot. "What is it?"

"Rabbit," Sam says.

"Rabbit?"

"Yes, King got it. So, I followed my grandmother's recipe, and it is ready to be fried there."

"No. Not me. That's something you can have for lunch. Let's go. That Home Town restaurant in Johnsonville."

"If that's what you want, then yes. The horse and carriage?"

"No!"

"The truck?"

"Sam!"

"Yes, dear. Your car. Oh, we're spoiled."

"I'm gonna spoil you, right out the door or into the carriage you love so much." She grabs his elbow, pulls him toward the door, opens it, and tries to lead him outside into the cold. He pulls back and dresses for the colder weather.

On the ten-minute drive, Fran briefs him on the day's activities in the hospital. Summarizing, she said, "It was rather uneventful. One stitching like the one I did on you. It was good to get back to work, and everyone wanted to know about our honeymoon trip. How was your day?"

"Uneventful. Except when King brought me the rabbit. On the way back from town getting your list of groceries, Sheriff Olsen was coming out our road. He wanted to know how it went there in Galveston. For ten minutes, I briefed him on it all.

"Well, here we are," Sam states as he pulls into the parking lot.

Sam finds a parking spot, and hand in hand, they walk toward the entrance and discover that they are number seven on the waiting list. "We could go home and enjoy the rabbit," Sam whispers to her.

"No way."

They sit in the waiting parlor along with the others. A couple next to them smiled as Fran sat next to the lady. A few moments passed, and the man leaned over and said, "Francinea and Sam, I recognize you from that young rascals event. I'm Peter Hostelier, and this is my wife, Vickie."

"Hi, Pete, Vickie. Yes, That's us. Francinea and I just got back from our honeymoon in Texas."

They all shake hands. Pete and Vickie congratulate them on their marriage. Then Vickie asks Francinea if she had time to change her name and status.

Francinea replies, "no, we haven't had time to get to the court yet. And when I do, I keep my name and add Sam's last name as my middle name. Why do you ask?"

Peter then says, "Well, on New Years Day, a new policy was instituted. When your number is called, you walk through the trellis, get scanned, and if all your information is not currently up to date, you will go to the back of the line."

"What?"

"While you're waiting, their system will then double-check your information. And, yes, if they find anything not current, they will not serve you. That's why Vickie asked if you had changed your name. Oh, I know, it's crazy, but everything else about the place is amazing. And the system does keep possible troublemakers out."

"You got to be pulling my leg," Sam says.

"No, I'm not. It's real," Peter replies. "Every bit of legal information about you must be correct: Married, single, address, phone number, email, employment, vehicle, licenses, yeah, everything must be current."

"Huh?" Sam states.

"Yes," Vickie says. "since then, the waiting time has diminished. It's easier to get seated and waited on, so we're glad about that."

Sam then says, "Okay, let me get this straight. Somehow, through the internet, I assume the information about each of us from the police, the courts, the state, probably our banks too, whatever. And that information is available to this restaurant, so now they keep our current status up to date. Hmm?. Well, I guess every obeying citizen will have a peaceful feeling while dining here."

"Yes, that's the way it is," Peter says. "Sorry."

"Well, thanks for telling us about this rather than having it shoved upon us when they call our number. Thanks, I appreciate it. Hey, how about joining Fran and me in the cabin sometime? You'll get to experience, for a bit anyway, what it's like to live without electricity. My grandfather was born in that cabin ninety-some years ago, and it's as it was then. Yes. Come on out. We'd enjoy the company."

Vickie says, "Yes, thanks, we'd like to." They exchange phone numbers and business cards. "Give me a call, Fran. A Saturday afternoon would be great."

Sam turns to Fran, "Well. That's it. We can't dine here." Sam stands, reaches for her hand, and they leave.

Two

"Well, honey, where would you like to go now?" Sam asks Fran as they settle down in the car.

"Oh, I don't know. I had my heart set on a nice quiet evening with you without having to cook anything."

"I did too. Whatever else they say about that place, the food, the service, the atmosphere is always terrific. We could get something to take home; a bugger, fries, and a shake. Or?" He pauses. "Ah, no, forget that."

"What were you gonna say?"

"Nah, forget it."

"No, tell me."

"The rabbit I was preparing."

"Oh, the rabbit. You found a recipe, followed the notes, and did all that for me. And what did I do, say? Yucko. Sorry dear, forgive me. Yes, let's go home."

Sam replies, "I love it. We've been married for two weeks, mostly in a hotel. You've only had two nights in the cabin, yet you called it home."

They start the short drive to the edge of Prairieville. Sam turns into the dirt road to the cabin. Stops in front of the porch and turns the headlights off. When Sam takes her hand, Fran opens the car door and is about to step into the cloudy dark evening. He points the flashlight at the porch stairs, opens the door, and leads her into the pitch-dark cabin. He lights the Coleman lantern hanging next to the door.

"Thank you," Fran says as she looks around the cabin. "How did you ever adjust to this life without electricity?"

"Oh, it wasn't easy. Took some time." Sam says as he adds kindling and wood to the stove as Fran watches and slowly feels the warmth of the pipes. She follows him to the fireplace, where he adds three wood pieces to the embers and blows on it. They sit close together on the couch, pulling a blanket over their knees and up to their necks. They silently watch the flames.

"I think I shared my ups and downs with you," Sam starts. "At first, it was like the excitement of going camping. My vow, dedicating it all to God, was the one thing that held me together. And I pinned those notes where I could read and remember that I made that vow."

"But Sam, there's a difference for me. You did not have a home you could go back to. I do. I could easily escape this and return to what I'm familiar with."

"You're right about that. But, moving here in mid-spring, the warmer weather made it easier, but still, the nights chilled down, and waking up, I felt the same as you did this morning." He leans forward to look into her eyes, concentrating on the fireplace's flames and warmth.

"Okay, let's put your home on the market," Sam says.

"No. Won't do that. It's for Meredith."

"She'll be married and going away to college this fall."

"Hmm?" Fran mumbles, "so, I guess I've got six, seven months to learn to accept this." she sighs.

"You do have that advantage. So, what say you? Pack your bags, and let's go. We'll make this a weekend experience."

"You wouldn't, would you?"

"No. I can't and will not. We've talked about this, and you agreed you'd do it. Yes, it's different, and periodically you will want the comforts. But you can do it, and I'll be here helping any way I can." Fran leans her head against his shoulder, and they quietly peer into the fire as the minutes pass.

"I feel better," she says. "Thanks."

Sam starts to get up. "You stay warm here, and I'll get you something to eat."

"No, stay here with me. I'm not that hungry anymore." He relaxes on the couch under the blanket, puts his arm around her, and pulls her close.

"Sam, the honeymoon was fantastic. Thanks. I sure hope Vickie and Peter will visit us soon."

"He told me he's enrolled in an environmental conference in Denver on the first of March." Sam feels her take a long deep breath and then touches her body slumbering. He leans his head against the top of the couch and closes his eyes.

Twenty-some minutes later, Fran suddenly jerks, looks at the clock on the wall, and Sam. She tosses the blanket off and rushes to the bathroom. Sam stretches, gets up, and adds wood to the fireplace. Fran appears in her pajamas and robe. "Honey, I've got an early appointment in the morning, so I'm going to bed. Are you?"

"I've got to let King out. Give me ten minutes." King is sitting at the door, wagging his tail. Sam opens the door and feels the brisk air. While King is out and Fran comforts herself on the bed, Sam adds wood to the stove and a few more pieces to the fireplace. Hearing the woofs of King, he goes to ket let King in, and the dog lacks up some water and then circles on his soft cushion by the couch. Sam carries the lantern to light the way to the bathroom. He pumps water into the tank above the commode and some into the sink. Turning the Coleman lantern off, he slides into bed.

In the morning, Fran, waiting for Sam to return with King, fixes herself a bowl of oatmeal.

"Not too bad out there this morning," Sam says as he enters the cabin. "Your car is warming, and you got a clear path to the car."

"Thanks. What are your plans for today?"

"Nothing pending," Sam replies.

"So, whatcha gonna do all day?"

"Not sure yet. I don't know. Haven't decided."

"Why not fix the door so King can come and go as he wants," Fran suggests.

"I wanted to do that before but can't install a doggie door. It would be against the rules imposed on me to keep everything as it was. And, wild animals would be able to use it too."

"Come on, honey. You're an architect. You could think of something." She pauses and then says, "Swing hinges. You know, hinges that swing out and in by the push. King would push the door open, just the bottom part, whenever he wanted, and the door would automatically close after he left."

"I thought about that," Sam replies. "But decided against it because of the wild animal part."

Fran says, "well, just an idea I had. Now, I've got to leave for a day in the office. Come by at noon, and we'll have lunch together."

"Sure. We can watch Joanna."

"Nah," Fran says, and Sam helps her take the few steps on the snow to her car, and she drives off.

Now what? King runs back to the porch. Sam looks at the door, wondering about changing the hinges. Inside, Sam calls the sheriff. "Hey, sheriff, could you come by sometime today? I've got an idea and want your input on it."

"Sam, sure. It'll be about ten."

"Thanks," Sam says and flips his phone closed. Here sits at the desk, inserts paper between the rollers, and starts typing.

My Cabin life 24

Now here I am with another perplexing situation.

Before Fran and I got married, I had no problem keeping busy one way or another in this lifestyle. I was my own man. Noone to please. No other human to bow down to. I could do what and when I wanted or needed to do. All this has changed.

But isn't that what love is all about? Love one another as He, who gave everything, loved us.

Now, I'm wondering what to do next this morning while Fran is at the office, and that whatever needs to consider our noontime lunch date.

And another problem. Fran wants King to be able to go out and in when he needs. Such as a doggie door. It disturbs her to hear King barking or jumping on the bed at night when he needs to go out, and to let him back in. King and his need to be able to go out when the need comes without disturbing me and/or Fran. Yes, it disturbed me at first, but I got used to it and learned to time it when I'd let King out.

Can't we do the same now?

Okay, the sheriff should be more familiar with that since he's been here long. Swing hinges could work, and those would not violate the demands of those bureaucrats that the cabin remains as it always has been. Would it?

Enough of this.

Sam pulls the sheet out of the rollers and slides it into the envelope containing all his notes. "Okay, King, let's take a walk. It's a nice sunny day, cold but not windy." Sam dresses for the weather with a leather jacket, hooded sweatshirt, boots, gloves, and cap. King runs toward the pier and stops to look at Sam, who points to his right. They enter the woods following the path started by his grandfather or perhaps great-grandfather. At the post with the red flag marking the end of his property and the beginning of the national forest, they continue walking further and further into the woods. Sam sees a deer about twenty yards in front of King, and off the dog goes, chasing it.

"Ah, perhaps we'll have venison," Sam tells the air. He follows a declining path trending toward the lake. Approaching a six-foot cliff down to the lake, he carefully sidesteps while holding onto branches and the exposed roots of trees till he stands on the narrow shore. He carefully steps onto the snow-covered frozen water and continues onto the ice. He stops, turns back to the woods, blows his whistle three times, and then a twenty-second loud blast. He looks to the left and right shoreline. No King. He blows the whistle again, and King appears, jumping off the cliff.

"Come, boy. Come!" King runs to get the treat, which Sam has in his open palm. "Good doggie. Where's that deer?" Sam says as he rubs the neck and shoulders of his pet. Sam and King walk the ice toward his pier a hundred yards away. *Maybe this afternoon, I could do some ice fishing.* Sam climbs onto the end of the dock as King trots alongside the ice to the shore, and off he goes to the gazebo and then the porch, where he barks at Sam, slowly walking through the ten-inch snow-covered ground. Standing on the porch, Sam tells his dog, "Okay, let's go in and warm up." He opens the door, and King shakes the wet snow off his body and starts eating from the dog food bowl. Sam adds wood to the fireplace and the stove. He places the coffee pot on top to warm. He soon hears a car approaching, and in walks the sheriff.

"Hi, cuz, good to see ya," Sam says to his cousin, the sheriff.

"So, what's so immediate on your mind this morning? I've only got a few minutes. Sorry, but I've been called to Johnsonville."

"Fran had an idea. If I changed the hinges on the bottom of that Dutch door to swing type so King could come and go as he pleased, would any of the wild animals be able to push it open?"

"Well, interesting idea. I guess it would depend on how much pressure was needed. I would be hesitant as foxes could almost as easily as King. Squirrels, skunks, rabbits, no, but larger wild ones could. Is that why you made this important call this morning?"

"Yeah, that's it, and nothing else pending. Thought I'd go ice fishing this afternoon."

"Be careful out there toward the middle where the water does not freeze as deep because of the currents. Go to that hardware store in Johnsonville, and they should have the hinges you're talking about. I've got to go. A deputy there needs my help. You remember that I'm retiring, right?"

"Yes," Sam replies. "I thought you'd be gone by now."

"The new sheriff elect starting date was extended until the twentieth, so I've had to delay the trip a bit. So I guess I'll see you when I return around the end of March."

"Thanks for stopping by, and have a great time enjoying that warm weather," Sam tells him as the sheriff leaves. King barks and follows the sheriff in his vehicle out of sight. A few minutes later, King returns to the porch. He jumps against the door. When Sam walks past the closet, he sees King standing at the window by the desk. He opens the door, and the dog enters. "King, we're going for a ride." Sam dresses warmly, grabs the key to his truck, and off they go. Sam turns right toward Johnsonville. Sam remembers his luncheon date with Fran and makes a U-turn to meet Fran at her office in Prairieville. He parks the truck and enters the office.

The clerk at her desk says, "Samuel, Doctor Ingersall is with a patient. She'll be available in a few minutes. Cup of coffee?"

"No thanks." Sam picks a magazine off the table and reclines in a cushioned chair. He turns page after page, scanning the headlines, the pictures, and the ads. Nothing of interest there, so he chooses National Geographic. He's about to read an article on the heating of the universe when Fran enters the lobby. Sam stands and embraces her.

"I've got an hour, Sam. Meredith put a pot of Chili on the stove before leaving for school this morning. Let's go." They leave the office, and Sam opens the truck's door. King paws on Fran's thighs and barks a few times, and Sam signals King to jump in the bed of the pick-up. Fran sits in the passenger seat, warmed by King.

"So, honey, whatcha been doing this morning?" Fran asks as he starts the vehicle.

"Took a walk," Sam replies as he pulls out of the office parking lot.

"That's all?"

"Well, no. The sheriff came by for a short visit, and we talked about those swing hinges you suggested for the door. I might do some ice fishing this afternoon. How was your morning?"

"Review of four patients."

"That's all?" Sam asks.

"You're copying me," she remarks.

"Of course. No one else here."

"Oh, it's back to those games of yours."

Sam starts singing: "Swinging low, swinging high, hinges high, hinges low." Fran joins him, and they repeat it together: "Swinging low, swinging high, hinges low, hinges high, Kings runs out, Kings runs in." And then Sam adds in his normal voice, "Skunk, possum, fox run in, and we run out."

"Did the sheriff suggest that may happen?" Fran asks. "And when does the new sheriff take over."

"The twenty-first."

"He said I need to talk it over at the hardware store about hinges with adjustable pressure. Here we are." Sam says as he pulls the pickup into her driveway. Sam leads King into her fenced-in backyard as Fran enters her house.

As Sam enters through the front door, Fran throws her arms around him, "I love you. Now let's eat." She leads him into the kitchen. She fills two chili bowls and buns and sets them on the kitchen table. She then opens the deck door, whistles, and puts a bowl on the deck floor. Fran joins Sam at the table.

They hold hands while Sam blesses the food.

"This is good," Sam says. "You said Meredith prepared this before school?"

"Yes. She has a habit of getting up early."

"Thank her for me. This is perhaps the best chili I've had." He takes another spoon full. Several minutes pass, enjoying the food. Fran reaches for Sam's bowl and puts them both in the sink.

"Time to head back to the office. Don't go to the hardware store today. Save it for tomorrow, and we could meet again for lunch while you're in town."

"Fran, my dear. You hurried thru this as if . . . well, like you didn't want to miss the opening of the latest . . . something."

"I've got an important appointment coming up. Let's go," Fran replies, quickly putting on her jacket. They leave the house, get into the truck, and Sam begins to back out of the driveway.

"Whoa," Sam says and stops. "Kings in the backyard." He runs to the fence, whistles, and King runs past Sam and jumps into the pick-up.

They arrive at Fran's office. Sam opens the door for her. "Thanks, honey. See you this evening." They hug and kiss, and Fran pets the dog.

"Bye. I'm going fishing. See Ya." Sam states and drives off.

Three

Sam arrives at the cabin. King jumps off the truck and runs toward the gazebo.

"Come, let's go fishing," Sam tells his pet.

Next to the pier, he tests the solidness of the ice at the shore. *Good.* He takes about thirty paces out from the end of the dock. He sets down his camp chair, a blanket for King, the pole, and pushes the snow away. Then he starts the process of auger drilling a hole in the ice. He removes the six-inch thick circular block of ice. *Good.* He baits the hook and drops the weighted line in the water. Holding the short pole, waiting for a bite, he looks around the area at the snowy mountains and the forest surrounding the lake, and King plays in the snow. He glances at his cabin, the gazebo, and the barn. He whistles for King as the dog appears to be venturing too far out in the lake. King comes back, grabs the treat, and lies on the blanket, chewing away.

It's quiet, the sun is shining its warmth, and the wind is somewhere else. He leans back in the chair and slides his ball cap back to let the sun warm his face. *Ah, that feels good.*

No bites, nothing. He raises the pole to bring the bait up and down. He waits. *Humm? Where's the fish? The sheriff suggested that this was far enough out in the lake. So, where are they?* He continues to move the line slightly. King rises and barks at a bird circling above them. *Are the fish doing the same? Swimming around the bait? According to all I've read about ice fishing, it shouldn't take this long. Am I not far enough out? I imagine it's dark down there as the ice and snow block the light from the water. Can the fish see anything, or are they hunkered down near the bottom? The water must be warmer at the bottom. Should I get a flashlight to shine its light down the hole?*

Sam reaches over to rub the neck and ears of his pet. Sam reaches down for a handful of snow and throws the ball out. King watches it crumble as it hits the snow ten feet away. Sam does it again, and King jumps, runs, and paws the ball as it hits, then barks again at the bird. Watching King and then the bird, Sam notices a drone circling the gazebo. *Who's doing that? And why?*

He feels a jerk on the rod. He raises the end some, lowers it, and raises it again, seeing the line drawn to the hole's edge and then deeper. He leans in, grabs hold of the line, and pulls it up. "Yahoo, a trout," Sam says as the fish struggles on the ice. He removes the hook and puts the fifteen-inch fish in the basket. He baits the hook and drops it into the hole.

"Two more would be good."

A half-hour later, Sam returns to shore with two fish and places them in his icebox. He glances at the clock and adds wood to the fireplace and stove. Feeling warmed, he decides to recline on the couch in front of the fireplace and read one of his grandfather's books. A few minutes later, Sam declares *I just can't get interested enough to read.* He dresses warm again, grabs two tennis balls, and goes out to sit on the porch. King is waiting for the ball to be thrown. Sam throws one toward the gazebo and another to the pier. As King chases the first, Sam's eyes wander back and forth around the porch.

"What's that?"

He steps on a footstool to examine the item. He pulls it out, looks directly into the lens, and says, "Eh, whoever you are who put this here, I'll find out, and the sheriff will deal with you for invading private property." He stuffs the small camera into his jacket pocket as King returns with the ball. Sam throws it again. When King returns with the ball, Sam points to the barn. "Come, let's go see the sheriff."

They get in the pickup and head east to town. Arriving at the office, Sam rolls the passenger side window halfway down for King. Opening the door, "Welcome back, Sam," the security guard says as Sam empties his pockets into the tray and walks through the scanner. Sam replaces the items in his pockets and enters the secretary's office.

"Hi, Sam. Have a seat," Sally, the secretary, says.

Soon, Sheriff Olsen comes out and greets Sam.

Sam hands the camera to the sheriff and is about to ask about it when the sheriff says, "So, you're here to return the camera?"

"Return it?" Sam quizzes. "That was yours?"

"Yes, Sam. Before you left on your honeymoon, I told you we'd install cameras around your cabin, just in case."

"Oh, I forgot."

"There's three more. One in a tree on your road to the cabin. One inside the barn and another on the gazebo facing the lake. It's your choice to leave them there or take them down."

"Well, thanks. I suppose there weren't any intruders."

"No. No people, but lots of animals. You need to get an animal control person to get rid of the possums under the porch."

"Oh, no. Possums?"

"Yes. I'm surprised King hasn't smelled that since you came back."

"If he did, he didn't make a fuss about it, to my knowledge."

"Well, that's it, Sam. Future plans?"

"Not really. Tomorrow, I'll go see what's happening at the Young Rascals school to check on the renovations. Oh, another question. I saw a drone flying around my area this afternoon. You know anything about that?"

"Haven't heard anything being non-compliant. No complaints from anybody."

"The cameras didn't pick up any of the drones?"

"Now, we didn't. They are pointed more at ground level. Kids are always messing with them nowadays. Good to have you back. Sam, take care. Please, no more calls. This new guy wants all the paperwork with the dots and dashes in its proper place. I have a few more days and will go south."

The sheriff turns and goes back into his office. Sam gets back into the truck and heads to the ice plant. He puts the ten-pound block of ice in the pickup's bed and is about to drive off but stops and calls George at the mill. George answers. "Hey Sam, I heard you were back, so I've scheduled you for a delivery tomorrow."

"Thanks. Yeah, and thanks for your help in keeping it from freezing while we were gone. Would you know anything about who could be flying drones in the area? I saw one circling my site today."

"Not specifically, but the high school kids were having some sort of a contest. Gene might know more about that, and the scouts play with them. Could be anyone."

"The one I saw was much larger than what the scouts use. Well, thanks. See you tomorrow." Sam then wonders. *Now, why did I thank him for keeping the cabin warm? It was Harry and Meredith who did it. Once in the morning before school, another after school. My memory slipping?*

"Well, Fran should be home in an hour or so." He drives to his road and stops at the mailbox. Removes the advertisements and dumps them in a sack behind the passenger seat. "King, no problem," he tells the dog, barking and sniffing the envelopes as he puts them in the basket. He continues down his snow-covered rutted drive to his cabin and parks the truck next to the porch. He carries the ten-pound block of ice inside and places it in the bottom section of the icebox. He adds two pieces of wood to the stove and three to the fireplace. Sam reaches into the icebox for the two fish he caught. He follows his grandmother's notes about preparing trout before cooking as the flying pan warms on the stove. The vegetables are mixed in a small pot and placed next to the frying pan. As he pumps water into a bucket, the movement of a car gets his attention through the window.

Fran's here. He bends down to hide behind the butcher block table.

The door opens, and Fran walks in. King runs to greet her. "Good puppy," she says, rubbing his neck. "Where's Sam?" Her eyes scout around the cabin. She walks to look past the closet and sees the bathroom door open. "Where is he? King's here, but where's he? She raises her voice, "Sam!" as she takes a few steps toward the table and closet. As she's about to push the curtain aside, Sam rises from his kneeling position behind the table and says, "boo!"

Startled, she falls off balance stretching her arms across her chest at the sudden interruption. She declares, "Oh, You scared me." She takes a deep breath and then adds, "Oh, I'm gonna boo hoo hoo you!"

He opens his arms for her embrace and pulls her in. "Good to see you. The food is just about ready. Got some trout and veggies."

She looks at the table, the condiments, the notes, the stove with the pan of trout, and a pot warming.

What's in the sack?" Sam asks, seeing the plastic bag in her hand.

"Oh, just some stuff I got on the way home. Here, I brought you the local paper. Go rest on the couch, and let me figure out how to cook on this stove. I want to do it." Sam sees her determination to learn this cabin life, so he does just that. He sits down in front of the fireplace to read the paper. King joins him on the couch. She sets the bag on the table and looks again at the stove, trout pan, and his grandmother's recipe. "Hmm?" she mumbles.

She removes the two styrofoam containers from the sack containing two rib eyes, one medium rare and the other well done, along with onion rings she brought from the Hospital. She softly whistles, and King raises his head, looks, and goes to the table when she gives him a treat. As King nibbles the treat, Fran removes the trout from the pan and places them in one of the containers. She strains the veggies warming on the stove, adds them to a container, and puts them in the icebox. She turns to the cabinets, chooses two dinner plates, forks, and knives, and places them on the table. She raises her voice, "This isn't as hard as I thought. So come and get it."

Arriving at the table, Sam sees the steaks, rings, and says, "Wow, this does look good."

"The one on the right is your favorite medium rare."

Looking at the stove, he asks, "Where's the trout?"

"Oh," Fran replies. "Forget them. I got your favorite steak."

"But the trout? You didn't trash them, did you?"

"Would I do that? Here, have the steak. It's still warm."

"The trout? Where are they?" He emphatically asks. "I spent over an hour on that frozen lake to catch them, and you threw them away. How could you?"

"Look and see," she replies.

 Sam flips the lid off the can, looks in the trash, and moves some items to see further. He sees the heads and tails of the trout and feels around, disrupting the basket. "It's not here. Where is it?"

"Da, da, da, da, there's the boo." Fran chuckles. "They're in the icebox. Yes, a boo on you. The hoo hoo will come later."

He straightens and looks at her with that big joyful smile. "Good one." He gives her a high five.

"Ya ha, I got the master of tricks. Ya, ha, I love it. Knocked him down some."

"Oh, come here. Just wait." He draws her in for a hug and kisses.

"Love you just the same," Sam whispers in her ear.

"Just the same as....when?"

"Tomorrow," Sam replies.

"Okay, honey, let's put all that aside till ... tomorrow and enjoy the food."

She holds his hand and prays over the food, adding, "Thank You for bringing Sam into my life. We do have our fun, Lord. And yes, tomorrow is another thing."

Sam adds, "Lord, thank you for everything. Looking at this steak, Lord, I see the entire process. Cows to be cared for as you instructed our ancestors, and they could enjoy the food within that cow. Thanks for all that and how you aided people through the centuries to make food for our bodies more tasteful. The trout too. Help us not to abuse any of your marvelousness in creation. Ah, Amen."

"Beautifully said," Fran tells him.

They sit at the butcher block table and enjoy the steak and onion rings as Fran relates her day's accomplishments. "An EMC brought one of the kids from the Rascals School to us. He had run head-on into the wall to catch a ball. Knocked some front teeth loose, bloodied his nose, and got a black eye."

"He's gonna be okay, though, right?"

"Yes. It was just surface wounds, except for those two front teeth. We treated the boy, and he's back at school."

"You know his name?"

"Patrick."

"Patrick?" Sam replies. "He's the kid that likes to play and work with King. Tomorrow, I'm going to that school to catch up on those renovations Jason and his group are doing, so I'll be sure to bring King, and I'll see how's he doing."

"Good. What time will you be there? We could have lunch together."

"I don't know. Whenever I'm ready, I guess."

"Yeah, that's been your life here, hasn't it? No schedules to keep. You did whatever was convenient whenever you were ready. But that's changing now, isn't it? Da, da, da, da, I'm changing that, right?"

"Well, I guess you are. In one sense anyway." Sam stands, leans in, and whispers in her ear

Four

Sam arrives at the school and parks the truck. "Come." King jumps out of the passenger seat and runs toward the playground. "Stop! King! Stop!" Sam yells and whistles. The dog stops, looks back at Sam, turns, and looks toward the playground around the corner of the building. And again, the dog looks at Sam, bent down on one knee. "Come here!" Sam tells his pet. King returns to Sam and gets a treat and a good rubdown. Sam takes a few steps to the entrance door, opens it, and King runs in first. They walk down the hallway and knock on Doctor Johanson's office door.

"Come in." Sam hears and opens the door. "Hey, Samuel. Good to see you. Congratulations on that honeymoon trip to Galveston. Sit down and tell me about it."

"Well, doc. It was fantastic, and thank you for helping the sheriff make those arrangements for us. We did have a great time. Superb is the best word. We got back a couple of days ago and are now back to business as usual, so I'm here to catch up on the rehab. How's it going?"

"Jason finished it two days ago. Come, take a look. "The doctor leads Sam and King into the hallway.

"I ought to let King out. Are the kids in the classrooms now?"

"Yes, go ahead and let him run around. The kids get a break." He looks at his watch. "In sixteen minutes."

"I heard about Patrick getting hurt. Is he doing okay?"

"He's doing well. Almost back to his ole self. And he'll be thrilled to see your dog again." The doctor leads them to the door to the fenced-enclosed playground. "A local company has volunteered to keep the playground snow-free." King excitedly runs out into the cleared playground.

Down the hallway, twenty feet, are four doors and then a fifth. The doctor opens the first door.

"Bunk beds." After a quick visual inspection of the room, Sam says, "Sure, why not. If I remember right, Jason said there'd be two to a room. There's enough room for individual closets, desks, and bunk beds. It looks good, and they've moved in already. Wow!"

"Yeah, Sam. The kids are happy about it too. No more of the twenty sharing one big room. The next three rooms are the same, but after that, there is a smaller room for one boy. Putting the bathroom closer than originally planned required a smaller room. Jason made the bathroom like one of the restrooms in the large stores: three stalls, sinks, and the showers." He opens the fifth door. "This room is designated for the captain of the boys."

"Captain?"

"Yes, Martha held an election to designate one of the boys as captain. His job is to help Martha in many ways and to lead them in games. The girls' rooms are about the same and have a captain. The cafeteria is at the end of the hallway, where we have movies and play games when the weather keeps them inside. Here take a look at it."

"Wow! Doc, I'm amazed. Jason finished all this in those two to three weeks I was gone?"

"Yes. We plan on rehabbing the other hallway. Jason has already customized two apartments for teachers. Sam, the program is growing. We've had to turn down requests because we don't have room for more."

"Is Jason around? I want to congratulate him in person."

"No, he's out." The doctor replies. "Sam, the kids will be getting their recess, so you should go out there and care for your dog."

"Yes. Okay. Thanks, Doc. This is fantastic. I'm available when you start on the other half." Sam opens the door to the recreation area free of snow and whistles when he sees King sniffing along the fence. King looks and runs to Sam. As Sam bends over to rub the ears of his pet, the bell rings, and the kids come running out. The kids, yelling and cheering, run to the slides and swings. Sam recognizes Patrick with a bandage across his nose. He's on the swing, and when he spots Sam holding King. He jumps off and runs to pet the dog.

"Hey, King, my dog," Patrick says as he rubs the ears and all over the dog. Sam hands Patrick a tennis ball. "Go get it!" Patrick says as he throws it hard to the fence. King takes off after the ball. "Oh, Mr. Guardus, thank you, thank you."

"How's the nose?" Sam asks as Martha approaches.

"My nose is fine. Wanna see?" He removes the bandage. "See, it's good."

Sam carefully looks at and around his nose. "Yes," Sam says. "It looks okay to me, so why are you still wearing the bandage?" King runs back with the ball. Patrick grabs it out of his jaws, tosses it, and follows King chasing after the ball.

Martha tells Sam, "He thinks he's more of a grown-up because he survived a tragedy. He uses the bandage as a sign to the other kids."

"Oh, Martha, the kids are blessed to have you as their teacher."

"Thank You, Mr. Guardyall, and it's good to see you again. Thanks for bringing your dog. They enjoy playing with him. And you got married, I heard, right?"

"Yes. And just got back from our honeymoon."

"Where'd you go?"

"Galveston, Texas."

"Will you be helping Jason rehab the other hallway?"

"Yes," Sam's flip phone rings. "Hi Fran, I'm at the school. It's amazing what they have done." He listens. "Oh, I'm sorry. Okay, give me a few minutes to get King, and I'll be on the way." he puts the phone in his shirt pocket.

"Sorry, Martha, but I promised Fran to meet her for lunch."

"You can leave the dog here if you plan on returning?" Martha suggests.

"Thanks. Yes, I'll be back. About an hour or so."

"Take your time. King can be part of our afternoon studies."

Sam leaves and meets Fran in the hospital cafeteria, five minutes away.

"Sorry, I'm late. Got caught up with the changes there at the school." He tells Fran nibbling on a sandwich.

"Sit down and tell me about it," Fran says.

"Patrick, the boy you ministered to after he ran into the wall. He's still wearing the nose bandage. He's got it so that it's high enough to cover the black eye."

"Why? It needs air to finish the healing process. I told him that and provided a copy of instructions to the one who brought him here."

"Martha says Patrick is using it as a token of war injuries."

"War injury? The kids only what, twelve, thirteen?"

"Martha's okay with it and says he'll get tired of doing it soon. Anyway, how's the morning for you? Sorry for being late."

"Thanks. I've been thinking of you all morning. You haven't been to the hardware store yet, have you? There's an antique car/truck lot next to it. I'll bet they'd be happy to buy that truck of yours. Give you a good price. Yes, hon, why not? Trade it in and get a new one. They're beautiful and full of all the modern conveniences."

"Huh? Sell the truck?"

"Sure, why not? What is it, seventy years old?"

"Yes, a 1952 Chevy. It was Grandpa's, and I'm keeping it. It just had an oil change. It's still in good condition. Runs great. Got two new tires last month. If anything, I'd give it a new paint job."

"Just a thought I had. A new one would ride so much more comfortably. For both of us on the next trip. Think about it."

"Next trip?"

"Somewhere around Easter. To Indianapolis to see Mark and Susan. Yeah, and you could revisit your old office."

"Now, that sounds good. Easter, Huh? But the pickup. No way. I'm keeping it. It's done me well, and the history behind it I want to keep too."

"Just a thought I had."

"You can go through the line and get something, but I don't have time to stay and watch you eat, so just stay here with me for five minutes, and then the schedule calls."

"Yes. Sorry again for being late." He reaches for her hands, squeezes them a bit, and asks for forgiveness.

"Sure, honey. This afternoon, I'm scheduled for an operation assist. A guy in his mid-sixties got trampled by a buck. Ooops! I'm not supposed to discuss our medical practices with anyone outside our staff."

"I'll not relate any of that. I'm now part of you, and you're part of me. We can trade our secrets with each other."

"Thank you. Well, duty calls. I should be back at the cabin about six. See you then." She rises and leans into Sam's hug.

Sam leaves the cafeteria and heads to the hardware store. Inside he follows the signs indicating door hardware. He looks at the selection of hinges, sees one, and picks it off the rack. A clerk is nearby. "Sir," Sam calls. "I'm looking for swing hinges that have adjustable pressure. I've got a German Sheppard, but it needs to be tough on smaller animals to push against and open the door."

"That's the one, sir. If a German Sheppard can't, nothing can. The pressure can be that much."

"How about a latch that would fall in place when it shuts? Nah, never mind."

"No need for that. That'll defeat the availability of your dog to come and go."

"Okay, Thanks. How about drones? Do you have them here?"

"No, we don't. Your best bet is online since there's not a Hobby Lobby store nearby."

Sam prepares to drive to the cabin with the hinges when he notices the ancient vehicles in the lot across the street. *Those are beautifully waxed. Oh, the history of those Model T's. There's a Chevy Bel Air.*

Sam finds a parking spot in the street and walks into the lot to look at the first car that caught his attention. The sign on the window describes it as a 1933 Model T.

"Good afternoon, sir," An elderly man greets. "A beauty, isn't it?"

"Yes," Sam replies. "Wow, When I came out of the hardware store, I paused and imagined what it must have been like to drive it back then, honking their horns at those using horses and carriages, no speed limits nor yellow lines. Does it still run well?"

"Oh, yes. Every vehicle here has been checked, checked, and checked before being displayed. Are you interested in selling that pick-up?"

"My pick-up?" Sam says. "No, I'm not. It was my grandfather's, and it suits me fine."

"We're interested in any vehicle from the 50's or earlier. I'm sure we could get you a fair price." The salesman pauses and takes a better look at Sam. "You were at the golf course where the Old Rascals held the convention, weren't you?"

"Yes, I was."

"I thought I recognized you. You're the one who's now living in Joshua Guardyall's cabin, right?"

"Yes. That's me. Samuel Guardyall."

"I'm Gregory Gambell. I was there too. Nice to meet you. Wow, I've got to tell Helen about this. Hey, you got a few minutes? Come in the office where it's warm."

"I'm not interested in selling my pick-up," Sam states.

"If you don't want to sell it, that's fine. I don't buy cars. I sell them for folks who can't or don't have the time or knowledge to do it. We negotiate a price, my mechanics do what is necessary, and I pay the owners and keep the commission when we sell it. Now, I'd like to chat about your grandfather."

"You knew him?"

"Yes, come on in." The older man leads Sam through the lot and into the office. "Have a seat. Could I get you a cup of coffee, water, anything?"

"No, I'm fine," Sam says. "Thanks."

The salesman sits behind a desk and Sam on a cushioned chair. "My wife Helen learned of your grandmother's cooking classes in their cabin, so she went and was thrilled she did. Learned a lot. We had just got married, so that must have been fifty years ago. She enticed me to go, and wow, Joshua saw my disinterest, and during a break, he enticed me to go fishing with him. We didn't have time then, so we arranged a later time. So, we sat on that porch and talked while the ladies were inside. He related his story of growing up right there, and, well, to get to his point, he asked me what I believed. Samuel, I was converted right there. I'll never forget it, and I owe him for his testimony that led to my life with Christ."

"Oh, bless the Lord God Almighty," Sam says. "Thank you. I don't know what to say. I just wanted to get a closer look at that Model T, and here I am, meeting someone who knew my grandfather."

"Hey, thank you for stopping here just now, as you brought those memories back. Two years later, I started this business. Our life has been fantastic. My wife Helen was a school teacher until she retired two years ago. I'm seventy-two and about to do the same. I'm giving it over to my grandson. So, I want to offer you any vehicle on the lot."

"What?"

"Yes, Samuel. I will. You're a good man. Your grandfather blessed me, and now, I want to bless you by offering any vehicle on these two lots. Yes, If you're interested in a newer vehicle, around the corner is where we have newer cars and trucks for sale. What would you have in mind?"

"It's not me, but my wife suggested I get a larger, more comfortable car for long trips."

"Bring her by sometime and let her choose, and she can have it. But as I said, It'll be yours, on this one condition. You stop here sometime this summer, invite my grandson to go fishing, and then share your testimony. He's a bit confused but searching."

"Wow! I've got to let this sink in. Thank you. I was captured by the Model T and stopped just to get a closer look at it. My head is shaking from the suddenness of this. I'll talk it over with Francinea. See you later, I suppose." Sam shakes his hand and leaves the office.

Driving back to the school, he prays out loud. "Lord, I thank You for directing me to this. To this small community where people know their neighbors, yes, where friendliness and respect are the norms. Oh, what a difference, Lord. Small-town life is fantastic. Thank You again and again. Now, direct my path and protect all I do. The drone, Father. What do I do? The possum?"

He arrives, parks his truck, and goes in to pick up King. He stops at the classroom and looks through the window. The kids are circled around Martha on the floor with their legs crossed and their hands on their knees. King is lying next to Patrick.

Hmm, I better not. Let them finish the meditation time.

Some time passes, and Martha opens the door for Sam. "It's okay now, Mister Guardyall. Come on in." The students clap twice as soon as Sam enters the room, followed by the pounding on their desks. Martha blows her whistle, and they stop. "You all remember Mister Guardyall," Martha tells the kids as Sam bends to welcome his pet.

"Woof! Woof!"

Holding the leash, Patrick restrains King.

"It's okay, Patrick. Let go of the leash." Martha tells him.

"No, no, no." Patrick loudly says. "He's mine. I don't want him to go."

"Yes, Pattie, let the dog go," Jack, the boys' captain, tells him.

The rest of the kids start the desk pounding as Martha walks up to Patrick, leans over, and tells the boy something. Patrick hands Martha the leash, and Sam treats his dog. "Sorry, Patrick, but it's time for King to go home," King follows Sam to the door, turns, and barks his bye-bye. They leave the school building and get in the truck. King's head is out the passenger window looking at the playground. Sam rubs the dog's back while waiting for a few cars to pass. Ten minutes later, he turns into his road, stops to retrieve the mail, and continues toward the cabin where George is unloading the chopped wood into the barn stall.

"Hey George, Thanks. I needed it."

George asks, "You asked about drones flying over the cabin. Some of our guys have encountered the same over our mill. One was seen coming out of the Federal Land Management area. One of our guys sent his drone, equipped to take pictures of that lake area. It was doing that, and then, blank, nothing. He believes it was shot down."

"Have you seen the pictures?"

"No. The guy who did it does not want to talk about it, as he's seen those drones over his house."

"Hmm. I'd sure like to talk to him. Something fishy is going on. Give him my phone number, or he could come by the cabin sometime."

"I'll do that, Sam. You should have enough wood for another week, but your horse needs some hay."

"Oh, yes. I was going to get some on the way back from Johnsonville but turned into my road instead, and here you are. Thanks, George. Back to those drones. I heard the scouts have been playing with them."

"Yes, we had a contest to fly them through circles over the central park playground. It was a race to see who could do it in the least amount of time. They enjoyed that, but that's about it. Now, whether any of them mess with them at home, I don't know. But their drones are just toys. Sam, The wood you have should last a week. If not, give me a call."

George gets in his truck and leaves, followed by Sam out to the main road. Sam continues to the farm, a few miles on the eastern side of Prairieville. Sam turns and proceeds down the quarter-mile dirt road to the farm. He parks in front of the large traditional red barn. King starts barking at the horses corralled in the fenced area.

"Mister Guardyall, how are you today?" Jeffery, one of the farmer's sons, greets Sam.

"Good. Just be glad when warmer weather hits."

"Yes, the horses want that freedom too. Okay, let's get some hay for you. Eight should do it." They load the rectangular bales onto the truck. Sam provides Jeffery with a check and is about to leave.

"Jeff, have you recently noticed any fairly large drones over the farm?"

"No, I haven't. Why do you ask?"

"Ah, I saw a good size one flying over my site. Just wondering."

"The scouts have had a contest recently, but it was over the school playground. The larger ones you mentioned are controlled by the feds and those they authorize because of their invasiveness of using cameras and recording mikes. I remember a news story, maybe three to four years ago, about a guy from China supposedly using a drone over the Hoover Dam, so the feds have cracked down on drone usage. But you know how news stories get twisted."

"Hmm. Interesting. The one I saw over my acreage was larger than any I've seen the scouts using."

"Tell the sheriff. You didn't get a snapshot of it, did you? But without proof, there's nothing they can do."

"Jeff, thanks. How's your dad doing after the operation?"

"He's recovering very well and ought to get up and out in a week or so."

"Tell him that we miss him in church."

"Yes, I will. Thanks. See you next week."

Sam leaves and heads back into town, where he stops at the veterinarian's office.

"Samuel, Oh, is King hurt again?" Penelope, the office clerk, asks.

"No, no, It's not King. I thought you might know how or who could get rid of a possum under my porch. Do you do that sort of stuff here?"

"No, that's a specialty." She types on her keyboard, prints a list, and hands it to Sam. "Here's a list of those wildlife animal control facilities that would handle that for you." Sam looks at the list of those, one in Johnsonville and others as far away as Denver. She then says, "Possums like the darkness and quietness, so some suggest putting a portable radio near where the animal enters and leaves, and perhaps a flashlight. Things like that drive them out. Then, install a wire fence to keep them from coming back."

"Well, thank you. Good. I'll try that." Sam tells her. "Meredith not here this afternoon?"

"No, Meredith quit a week ago."

"She did?"

"Yeah. Do you want a job?"

"A Job? Ha. No thanks. King is doing great and seems to stay away from skunks," Sam tells her as he turns to leave. "Well, God bless you and all you do to help the pets. See you again. Hey, I just had another thought. When I catch the possum, I'll bring it here, Okay?"

"No. no. No. Take it to the Federal Land. They like to protect the wild animals."

"Wow. I'd like to send that skunk too." Sam and Penelope chuckle. He leaves and starts to head back to the cabin. *Hmm? Fran will be home in a half-hour.* He stops at the diner.

"Good afternoon, Sam," Joanna greets him, leads him to a booth by the window, and then sets a glass of water in front of him.

"Afternoon!" Sam states. "I'm here to get two of those chicken breasts smothered with mushrooms and your delicious onion rings. To go."

"Ah," Joanna replies. "I can straighten the rings so you can tell Fran that you did your best."

"Ha, then it'd be onion halves."

"Sam, When you get the possum, bring it here, and I'd be glad to make a possum steak for you." A lady enters the diner. "Hi Betty, June coming? Grab a table back there." Betty looks at Sam and keeps walking.

Looking back at Sam, "Okay, I know that look. Your order will be ready in six and a half minutes."

"Thanks. Tomorrow, I'll open the door and kick the possum in, and you can deal with it then." Joanna quickly removes the glass of water and leaves the table.

"Yes, Lord, small-town life is interesting," Sam says as he watches Joanna's gum-chewing jaw. While waiting for the meals, Sam pens a note to Betty.

Five minutes later, Joanna brings him the two meals. "It's on me today. Seriously, it's a honeymoon gift, and congratulations again. Thanks, Sam, for dropping in. You're always a delight to mess with, and I wish others would loosen up a bit."

Oh, Thanks, Joanna. Here, I penned a note for Betty. But run fast before she reads it. Joking again. I heard she was promoted to full-time status, and that's all, a congratulations note to her. And here is a note for you, but wait for me to leave."

"Don't stay away too long," Joanna says. "Bring Fran in next time, and God bless you in this new life."

Sam leaves the booth, takes the sack, and drops a ten-dollar tip in the jar at the check-out counter.

Five

"Whatcha been doing, Sam?" Fran asks as Sam enters the cabin.

"Been cleaning the stall and adding hay for the horse."

"Is that all? It's ten-thirty."

"No. It's a beautiful day, the sun shining, so I snow-blowed the garden area. The horse may want to run a bit to enjoy the warming weather, so I put some hay out there." After removing his jacket, cap, and gloves, he pulls Fran in for a hug. "And good morning to you. How did you sleep?"

"Surprisingly, very well. Thanks. Did you eat anything?"

"Had a biscuit and coffee. Are you hungry?"

"Not after that salad, steak, potato, and roasted turnip greens last night, and we still have some left over. But, I will want lunch, so let's go to my house and learn more from Meredith about why she quit the nursing career."

"I thought she got more interested in a writing career."

"That's what she said, but I'm sure there's always more to the story. Let's go then."

"Now? Can't we wait a bit? There are a few other things I need to do."

"Like what?"

"I don't know. I came in to warm up a bit and think about it. But there's always something to do around here, like bringing more wood to the porch. Testing the ice. Clean the gazebo area. Remove snow from the roof. Check the fireplace chimney. Daily devotions and catch up on reading Shakespeare."

"You're not reading Shakespeare. Where did that come from?"

"Okay, let's go. Horse and carriage?"

"Sure, you use that. I'll drive my car and meet you on my way back after talking to Meredith for an hour. Then we'll use the pickup and get a new truck for you. I saw one I like. How about you? What do you want?"

"I'll let you choose between two."

"Only two? I know he's got more than two on that lot."

"Oh, did I leave the twenty out?" Sam jokes.

"I'm gonna leave you out," Fran replies. She looks at the thermometer and starts dressing for the cold weather. Heading to her house in Prairieville, Fran says, "Honey, I know I've asked you this before, but really when, how did you start that? What I call the word game of yours. You know, tossing the conversation back, based on one word."

"It was with my Angelia. She started it on me. Oh, she was good. She was always making up funny alternatives. She called me Mas one day.

"I said, Huh?" She told me If my ears were right to left, I'd hear the word, Sam."

"What? That doesn't make sense."

"You're right. For her, that was the purpose of it."

"You said, my Angelia. Did you own her?"

"Yes, she was mine, just like you're now mine, so fix me some pancakes, shine my boots, and . . . "

"I'll shine your …," she declares as Sam takes his eyes off the road to look at her, and they start laughing. Arriving at the house, Sam leads his dog to the fenced-in backyard as Fran opens the front door.

"Meredith, we're here." She walks past the kitchen and dining room to her daughter's bedroom. She knocks twice, waits, and then enters. No Meredith. She goes through the living room and opens the patio door, and there is Sam and her daughter holding a leash to a small dog sniffing King's nose.

"Hi, Mom. I got a puppy. I've named her Pretty."

"When did you get her?"

"She was a gift by the Vet when I left."

"Yes, we heard you quit," Fran replies. "But why? You were doing well there and enjoyed working with pets and ministering to their medical needs."

"I told you I'm changing careers. Now I've got time to write. The principal has put me in charge of the student's monthly newsletter as the editor and columnist." She unties the leash, and Pretty runs after King circling the yard.

Fran says. "Are you sure about this? You were doing such a great job there and getting a start in nursing."

"Mom, I am. Dad was a journalist, so it could be that I have more of his genetic DNA than yours."

"Well, I'll be," Fran says. "He was good. And a great photographer too."

"Thanks, Mom. Please don't worry. I'll get you a copy of an article I wrote last week." She enters the house, gets it, and hands an envelope to her mom. "Just five pages. But, please wait until you return to the cabin, as there's a bit about you. Harry is all for it, and did you hear he dropped the football scholarship at Colorado U? He'd rather concentrate on carpentry than football for ten years, along with possible injuries."

Sam replies, "The Broncos had even scouted him. Wow! Fran, we're gone two weeks, and look what's happened."

"I'm stunned," Fran says, pulling her daughter in for a hug, "I love you. Thanks for sharing this with me. I'm here for you all the time. Can you spare a few hours, and we'll eat something in Johnsonville, where we are getting Sam a new truck?"

"Harry's bringing some take-out. So, don't go yet."

"Sure, there's no rush," Sam replies. "Mr. Gambell will be there all day." They go inside the house, and after removing her jacket, Fran makes some coffee. Sam leans back on the recliner as Meredith goes to freshen up in the bathroom.

Fran hands Sam a cup of coffee. "There you are, master, your coffee. As your servant, what else can I do for you."

"Thanks. Ah, my boots. Take them off and massage my feet."

"Yes, sir," Fran says. "Left or right one first?"

"Hey, that bit about what Angelia said about my ears being right to left. At the time, I never thought much more than its nonsense. We read sentences left to right, but the original Hebrew language is written right to left. So Angelia was partially correct. Now put those three letters 'mas' on paper. The Jews, reading letters right to left, would see sam."

"Humm?" Fran softly says. "You started to study Hebrew once, didn't you."

"Yes, my grandfather has a book on Hebrew. Shortly after moving here, being curious, I picked that up one day and began. That's….."

"Mom, Sam, Harry is here." Meredith interrupts, opens the door, greets Harry, and leads him into the living room.

Sam rises and shakes Harry's hand. "How you doing?"

"Very well," he replies and hugs Francinea. "If I knew you'd be here, I would've brought two more sandwiches."

"We surprised Meredith, too. We're on our way to Johnsonville." Sam is going to get a new truck."

"That's a surprise," Harry says.

Meredith brings the sack into the living room and sits beside Harry on the couch, facing Sam and Fran. "Mom, you don't mind, do you?" she says.

"No, enjoy it. Harry, we heard you've dropped football and the scholarship. Is that right?" Fran asks.

Sam watches Harry take a sip of his drink and says, "That looks like a beer, is it?"

"Yes. It is," he replies, adding, "I'm eighteen, old enough to drive a car and vote, so why can't I?"

"Ask the governor," Sam states.

"Yeah, and if I made a fuss about it, they'd raise the age of legally driving to twenty-one or ban the sale of beer altogether, and those over twenty-one would be upset."

"Hmm?" Sam says. "Round and round it goes." Sam then adds, "On another subject, what type of drone are the scouts using? I saw one larger than those the scouts use flying over my cabin the other day."

"We use mostly the small toy type anyone can get at a hobby store. The other eagle scout and I have one with a camera. The most expensive ones also have a microphone to pick up sounds, and the battery lasts longer." He takes a bite of his sandwich, chews it, and then adds, "Many police and fire departments use those. They cost in the neighborhood of three thousand and up. I think there's one with a solar panel, so it can fly longer distances when the sun is out."

"Very interesting, thanks," Sam says. "How about the football scholarship? Why did you drop out? Ah, finish your sandwich. It looks good."

Harry says, "I read an article about a company now building one with six propellers, powerful and large enough for a pilot to sit inside, and it will still be classified as a drone."

"Wow. That may have been what I saw over the cabin."

"It's not out yet. The article said perhaps another six months or longer after months of testing. And then it'll be only available for police or FBI inspections."

"Harry," Fran says. "The football scholarship. Meredith told us you canceled it to go full-time carpentry."

"Yes, I did."

"Mom," Meredith says. "Harry may feel he's getting the third degree, so drop it."

"Mer, It's okay," Harry says. "I've been in touch with a professional interested in having an apprentice and possibly taking over the company. The guy thinks he may partially retire in a few years. He's looked at what I've done and considers me among two others."

"That may be your ticket to the future," Sam says. "The guy I hired as an apprentice ten years ago is now running the company I had built from scratch."

"Football, no more," Harry says. "The season is over, and that desire is too. Think about professional sports. The salary and the fans are great, but the team owner has you under his thumb. He owns you. He can trade you back to the minors or home anytime and wherever. The more I thought about it, the less appealing it became. So goodbye to football and hello to woodwork."

"Sam," Fran says, focusing on Sam. "All this happens when we are gone for two weeks. Perhaps we should leave for another two weeks."

"Yes, the honeymoon was fantastic," Sam says. "But being home is rest, comfort, and peace. You've heard the phrase: it's good to get away and better to get home."

"You said peace," Fran says. "When your mind is captivated by a mechanical bird you imagine is spying on you, is that peaceful? Nope, If I didn't have a profession to work at, we'd be heading south again in that new truck you're getting this afternoon. Peace is getting up when I want, calling the desk to bring me lunch, and…."

"Fran, this is real peace, knowing that the peace of God transcends all our natural understandings and guards our heart and mind in Christ Jesus. I'm not anxious about that drone. I'm asking questions. It's that curiosity God gave us, and I want to know who and why. Someday, I will get answers.

"A short time after coming here, I was sitting by that stream feeding the lake and quietly admiring the beauty and wonders of the area. It was a beautiful day, with a few fluffy clouds dancing over the mountaintops.

Hearing birds singing in the distance, I started singing, "When peace like a river." Now that hymn is a story of peace in spite of a horrible tragedy."

"The author, Horatio Spafford, had planned to take his family on a European trip. His business held him back a couple of days, so he sent his wife and daughters ahead, arranging to meet up with them a day or two later in England. Their ship ran afoul with another and quickly sunk, drowning his daughters, but his wife somehow survived.

"Now, when I learned about the sudden death of my wife, I couldn't handle the loss and became a drunk. Fran and Meredith, I can only imagine the feelings you experienced when hearing the news about your husband and father. Feeling the presence of God during those times enables us to continue. And that's how that hymn came to be."

"Come on, let's sing it together, okay?" He looks at Fran, Meredith, and Harry, leans his head back, and starts singing.

"When peace like a river attendeth my way,
when sorrows like sea billows roll;
whatever my lot, thou hast taught me to say,
It is well, it is well with my soul.

Though Satan should buffet,
though trials should come,
let this blest assurance control:
that Christ has regarded my helpless estate,
and has shed his own blood for my soul.

It is well … with … my soul,
It is well. It is well … with my soul."

Fran moves next to Sam and leans her head against his shoulder. "Thank you," she softly says.

A few minutes later, Sam says, "Let's get back to life as it is. Meredith, your mom and I need to go."

"Not yet, honey," Fran states. She grabs his hand while leaning against his shoulder, resting and closing her eyes.

Six

"Sam," Fran says. "I'm okay now. We'd better go. Where's Meredith and Harry?"

"Harry returned to work, and Meredith is outside with her puppy."

Fran gets up, stretches, and says, "Thanks, that nap felt good. Warm up the car while I say bye to Meredith."

"Gotcha and I'll get King from the side gate."

They don their jackets and boots for the cold. After starting the car, Sam walks to the fenced-in backyard. "King!" he hollers, and King runs to the front yard, stops, and looks back at Sam.

"No! In here," he tells the dog as he opens the car's back door. Seeing Fran coming out, Sam opens the passenger side door. She slides in and gets a woof and a lick from King.

They pass through town on the way to Johnsonville. Sam drives past his entrance road when Fran says, "How about the truck? I thought you were trading the truck in for the new one."

"No, I'm keeping it. A gift from grandpa."

"If that's what you want, then ok," Fran says. She leans toward Sam. "I'm still a bit upset about Meredith's decision."

"You are? After what seemed like a definite medical career following in your footsteps, I understand how that would surprise you."

"Well, I hope she doesn't go the same way as my late husband. He was enticed by the income promised. That's too dangerous, a lot more so now with what's happening around the world."

"You got that right," Sam replies. "Well, here we are." He parks the car and leads Fran into the lot. "What color would you prefer?"

Gregory Gambell greets Sam as Fran stops and looks at a four-door, deep red-toned Honda pickup. "Mrs. Guardyall, get a good look at the insides here." He pushes a few buttons, and the passenger side door opens. She gets in, moves around on the seat, leans back, and focuses on the dashboard. Gregory opens the driver's side for Sam. "Start it."

Sam presses the start button.

"Sounds smooth," Sam says. "What year is it?"

"A twenty-twenty, with only eight-thousand, three hundred miles on it. Let's take it for a ride, Sam." Gregory settles in the back seat. Out of the lot, Sam takes them through the streets of Johnsonville and turns to go down some rough dirt farm roads.

"Sam," Gregory leans forward and tells Sam, "turn right at the next intersection, and you'll see how it handles the hills."

After the up and down of a steep hill, Sam says, "It seemed effortless."

Back in the lot, Sam asks Fran, "Well?"

"It's beautiful and rides very comfortably. I like it."

"But how about that Jeep over there?" Sam points at a black four-door Jeep.

"No. Why would you want a Jeep?"

"It'd be easier to find in a parking lot," Sam answers.

Fran then asks Gregory, "You could paint this one in a way that would make it easier to find, right? Like rainbow colors for Sam."

Gregory looks at Sam for a reaction, then at the smiling Fran.

"Ha," Sam chuckles. "This one looks good, Gregory."

"You like that. But hang on. A lady friend called me after you left the other day. Her husband passed into glory a few weeks ago, and she has no need for a vehicle and told me to take it and get whatever I can for it. The mechanics have checked it, and no problems were found. It seems to be in perfect condition." Gregory leads them into the shop when they see a beautiful black four-door GMC truck.

Fran says, "Wow, it's a beauty."

Sam gives it a thumbs up.

"We've got another day or so to check it completely. So. If everything checks ok, we'll deliver it to you then. There's no rush for you, is there?"

"No, not really." Sam looks at Fran for approval.

"Sure, no problem," Fran agrees.

"All right, let's go in and sign the papers," Gregory says. "I promise you it'll be ready as if it was new. We've been doing that since we opened the shop."

In the office, Gregory tells Fran about how Sam's grandfather led him to accept and believe the gospel. "A few years after that, I was able to open this business, and life has been fantastic since then, with only one regret. I was never able to repay Joshua. I'm retiring soon, Fran, so this car is yours."

Fran says, "Gregory, we're doing okay financially. Not a big problem for us, so let's agree to a payment from us."

"No!" Gregory responds. "Joshua and I would meet once a week to read the Bible together that first year I became a Christian. I owe him big time. So, please accept my gift, and I pray it doesn't make you feel guilty."

On the way back to the cabin, Fran says, "It'll be perfect for our trip. Will you want us to include King on our vacation?"

"Haven't thought about it. We can wait for that decision. When is Easter this year, anyway?"

"Three months from now, mid-April. Let's sit by the fireplace and discuss our plans."

After Sam refurbishes the stove and the fireplace, he refreshes their coffee. They're comfortably settled on the couch, watching the flames rise as the wood catches fire.

Fran asks, "What did you do on a Saturday afternoon to pass the time?"

"Hmm?" Sam says. "Well, I arrived in late March when the weather was warming, and the snow had already melted. At first spent lots of time exploring the area, the forest, the town, and did some fishing. Fishing is a great way to be busy, with time to reflect on whatever as you wait for the catch. And, of course, reading books that my grandfather had collected. It took some time to get accustomed to candlelight reading at night. The first week was like a camping trip, yet knowing this would be my life. When the remembrances of 24/7 electricity surfaced, I would be brought back to reality. It wasn't easy, though. When sitting by the stream one day, watching the clear water flow over rocks. Oh, how clear and beautiful it was. I put my fingers in the water, and the thought came. That's life. We don't feel the past or the future, only the here and now. I enjoyed watching the birds and the other animals. I saw an eagle circling over the lake, slowly getting closer and closer to the surface, and then, zoom, it went down into the water and rose with a fish hanging off its claws. Wow. I had never before paid any attention to the intricacies of nature with my new eyes opened to God's creation."

"Fran, am I boring you?"

"No, it's interesting. That meeting with Jim's class was when I got intrigued by you. They were right about you becoming a teacher. Why didn't you?"

"Designing buildings was my gift, and I'm glad I got with it."

"Go on," Fran says.

"Ah, where was I? One day, I followed that stream inland up the slope. There I watched a beaver gathering limbs to add to his dam. I guess he didn't like the swift-moving waters of the stream, so he was making a pond of still waters.

"God, how did you do this I asked the air. Soon an answer came, not out loud but in my inner ear, my heart: 'I did it for you to enjoy.' "But skunks," I asked, "and rattlesnakes too. Mosquitoes? Wasps and poison Ivy. Why those?" Then my inner parts heard: 'You're inquisitive, so you tell me why.' Sam stops and stares into the rising flames.

"Oh, what a blessing to be warmed by burning wood. So many types of beautiful trees put here for our benefit, some with fruits, some producing nuts, and, later in the year, displaying wonderful fall colors. Their leaves drop, becoming fertilizer as the trees go to sleep over the winter.

"Seeing all this come alive in my heart from then on, any acceptance I may have had about everything evolving disappeared. Our scientists say that's an easy answer, a myth. They continually hit us with the notion that billions of years ago, a big bang of atoms and molecules bumped heads, split apart, and formed into more extensive and complicated ones, eventually evolving into moons, planets, and the sun. And on and on, they tell us, simpletons. The Sun shined, rains fell, and plants started to grow, and then those atoms formed into small animals, then into more varieties over billions of years, evolving into lions, bears, cows, camels, and horses moving on four legs. And possibly from there, those apes, or monkeys, learned to walk upright on two legs, and instead of barking and howling, this new animal form started talking in words. So, here we are, they postulate, possibly 3.5 billion years later.

"Oh," Sam says. "I'm boring you."

"No, no. Go on." Fran says. " I enjoy hearing you use that gift to teach. You got to take the pastor up on his offer. Now, continue with what you call rambling. It's a subject nobody likes to discuss, but I do."

"The sun, moon, and stars have evolved from whatever? Are they still evolving, larger, smaller, or will they eventually burst apart into two or more?"

"Can't be proved, can it? And the earth still rotates on the same axis feeling like a roller coaster Ferris wheel going round and round."

"The Bible became not a novel, but a real historical read, and I read it with new eyes and heart. History does not change."

Sam looks at Fran. Her eyes closed. She was napping. He leans back against the couch and closes his eyes.

A few minutes later, King enters through the new doggie door and slops up water from his bowl, waking Sam and Fran.

"Sorry, hon," Fran says. "I shouldn't submit to a nap so easy."

"I did too," Sam says, as King jumps on the couch, wanting some warm hands to rub his tummy.

"Ah, these naps came more often when moving here, and getting used to and managing the necessities of cabin life. I have less to worry about in the world of daily technological life by keeping up with the latest new gossip."

"Back then, I'd spend the first half-hour or so reading the latest news, wondering or trying to determine which was biased and which was factual. In construction, I had to keep up with the new devices that were taking over the older, tried, and true methods we had used for decades. It was hard to keep up. Now, without electricity, means no computer to scan the news each morning. No TV to watch, none of that stuff to manage my focus on what everyone else is doing. And, during storms, preparing for the possibility of power stations losing their grid. Now, I'm always prepared. Candles, Coleman oil lamp, oh, and flashlights. Fireplace for heat, as it's the usual daily thing, and I love it."

Sam pauses to look at Fran snuggled up next to him. " And, Fran, I pray you'll feel the same way."

Fran says, "I hope to and want to, but my job of being in the world forty or more hours each week hopefully doesn't weaken my desire to adjust to this life. Now, what are you discovering about that drone disturbing your peace?"

"Well, I want to know who was in control, that's all. Was it just a kid playing around, or was it someone spying? If so, why?"

"Ah, you hungry?" he asks.

Fran replies, "No, not a bit. Like you said, we look at the clock to see if we're hungry. That's so true in our lives. We've been conditioned to eat by the clock. Let's go lay down under the blanket and sleep to whenever."

"Yep, why not." Fran rises and goes to the restroom as Sam adds wood to the fireplace and stove, blows out the flames of candles, and crawls into bed next to Fran, who then says. "Sam, reconsider the pastor's offer to lead a Bible study. Pray about it."

Seven

After the church service, Fran and Sam invited Pastor Thomas and his wife to dinner to further discuss the program the pastor had mentioned to Sam.

Sitting in the circular booth in the diner, Fran says, "Yes, Sam would love to lead a weekly bible class."

"That's great, Sam. Thanks," the pastor answers.

Ruby, the waitress, brings them coffee and hot tea for Mary.

Sam has been looking around the diner, wondering. He asks Ruby, "Where's Joanna?"

"She's taking a few days off."

They tell Ruby what they'd like, and she leaves, "It'll be ready in ten." Looking at the pastor, she says, "Sorry, I missed church this morning, but I had to fill in for Joanna."

"That's okay," Pastor Thomas says as Ruby leaves the booth.

"Now, Sam, are you sure and willing to accept my offer?"

"Well, ah, yes," Sam replies. "I've been giving it more thought, but again, like I so easily do, once I get going, the rambling takes over. At that fiasco in the cabin that Gene arranged, I was to discuss life in the cabin for ten to fifteen minutes, plus a little history, and I kept going and going, and Gene had to declare an intermission to give the kids a break."

"It wasn't like that at all," Fran says. "I thought you had studied hard and rehearsed it over and over to get it right."

"Sam, this is different. These adult men have other things to do, so it'll be a one-hour program. Group discussion type. They'll be watching the clock."

Mary, the pastor's wife, says, "Ah, back to Joanna. She's rebelling against her parents, who want to shut the diner down on Sundays. Joanna says it'll dramatically reduce her income."

Sam then says, "Why would they do that? This town depends on it for family and friends Sunday lunches. Look at how many are here. She's already lost quite a bit since Chick-fil-A opened."

"Her parents had moved to Montana over a year ago," Mary says. "They made a deal with Joanna to run the diner as if it was hers. She's done a terrific job, too, but she says that she will lose much more without the Sunday crowds."

"Oh, Why do they want to shut the place down on Sundays?" Sam asks,

The pastor answers, "After moving to Montana, her parents became involved with a group that held their church services on Saturdays."

"Seventh Day Adventists?" Sam asks.

"I'm not sure it is a part of that denomination or independent like us." the pastor says. "A couple of our elders have seriously considered all ten commandments as recorded in Exodus twenty, including the eighth, ninth, and tenth verses. Keep the Sabbath holy, no work whatsoever. God rested after six days and commanded the Jews to do the same to keep the seventh day holy.

"Sam, this would be one of the subjects I'd like you to dig into in one of the bible classes: The Ten Commandments and how replacement theology dismissed it through the years."

"Oh, my," Sam says. "I've always wondered why there are so many denominations. I had trouble with it. It seemed like a battle over who was right. Each group says you should be part of our church because it's theologically correct. And I wondered, why? Don't they all use the same book?"

Fran says, "It was a thorn in my side too for a while, but then I just made a decision, and glad I did. The fellowship with the others was great."

"But," Sam says. "It's like, well, similar to our desires. Some like spaghetti and meatballs, some prefer lasagna, and on and on it goes with our choices of ice cream flavors. One day back home, I counted the number of restaurants and fast-food drive-thrus in one square mile. Eighteen. At one intersection, there were three restaurants and six fast-food joints. Two pizza places. Oh, there I go again, off our subject again."

Sam pauses and then continues. "I have read Josephus, the historian, penning history back in the third century. I found it intriguing. I think the Roman emperor Constantine and the council of Nicaea accepted and established Easter on Sunday, three days after Jesus's crucifixion. And, so, we have church services on Sunday."

"Sam, you're a good historian," Pastor Thomas says. "And, yes, from my understanding, It was way back during the Roman days that Constantine accepted Sunday as the seventh day of rest. It might have appeased those who worshiped what they called the

Sun god. That's where the name Sunday came to be. People don't realize that we tend to repeat history when we forget or negate history. And now that we've got all this technology, we think we're so much smarter than previous generations."

Ruby sets their meals down and refreshes their coffee and tea. "Enjoy it. We thank you for coming. Be back in a bit with the dessert of today."

They hold hands as the pastor prays over the food. "And, Lord, we ask a special blessing and guidance on Joanna. Thank you. Amen." He looks at the dishes and says, "Okay, looks good. Thank You, Lord. Sam, I've read some of your grandfather's notes and summaries he presented to the church. You've got the same gift. So, when would you like to start?"

"I don't have a calendar. Well, I didn't, but now married to Fran, she reminds me and keeps me up to date. So, ah, You pick a time. But if you don't mind, I'd like to just sit in the first meeting as an observer."

"Sure, Sam. I'll get it started, and perhaps the men would initiate hearing your observations. You're well-known to most of them. Okay, that's settled, so let's put all that to rest and enjoy these delicious meals."

After dinner, Sam and Fran stop at her home to wash some clothes. While Fran is taking care of that, Sam uses her computer.

"Well, what did you find so interesting?" Fran asks.

"The Pastor mentioned those who worshiped the sun way back in the days of Noah and Lot. Interesting, so I looked it up. I imagined what it could have been like to live three to five thousand years ago, depending on the sun for light. When the sun descended, all they had was the light of the moon. I've experienced that by moving here. Did they have candles to see inside their cave or tent? Fires? Was it only small branches of trees they could break off? No chainsaws to cut the tree down. None of our modern tools to use."

"Yes, it'd be easy to bow down to the sun for light and warmth, and when the clouds came, you may have cursed it. Ancient history is still a mystery; I guess it'll always be for us. Stonehedge in England was built in a circle, as were many of those ancient structures. Was it another type of sun worship? The shadows from the pillars following the sun's movement? Was that their hour clock? If so, those ancient folks were not as dumb as we think they must have been because they didn't have cars and TVs."

"Well, honey, It's almost three. What now?" Fran asks.

"I want to print these articles first. Do you have paper and ink?"

"I think so."

Sam hits the print button. "This will take some time. While it's printing, let's play a game. Yeah, you know how to play chess, right? So let me beat you in a quickie."

"I can't play chess. I told you that on the honeymoon."

"Checkers?"

"No! Let's watch something on TV. Come on." Fran grabs his wrist and leads him into the living room, where they get comfortable on the couch. She turns it on and scrolls to a travel program. "Oh, I know that look of yours," as commercials appear. "You want sports, don't you? Sam, dear, relax. It's about a German couple detailing their walk through the Alps. You never got overseas, did you?"

"No, never did," Sam says. "Angelia and I spent our vacations camping by lakes. We had a Winnebago."

"That's not camping," Fran says.

"Well, not in the same sense as sleeping in a tent. But we still called it camping out. One of the best was in Wisconsin, near the Wisconsin Dells. I wish we had gone to places like Switzerland, Greece, or even Israel. There's so much history there."

"We could do that sometime," She says. "My first husband and I did. He was sent to Nurenburg to film a documentary about the concentration camps the Nazis had built for the Jews. The company arranged for a German guide to lead us to Auschwitz in Poland. And after that, we went to Dachau and Buchenwald. Wow, seeing those barracks and visualizing those horrific conditions the Jews were subjected to, I'll never forget it. He had taken thousands of pictures and recorded conversations with a few of the survivors, now in their nineties. He won a prize for one of the best documentaries ever televised. After he had sent all of his info back to headquarters, they gave him several days off, and we drove down to Switzerland to relax."

"You're proud of him. I'm sorry for your loss. If I remember right, you said he was killed in Afghanistan while accompanying our troops on a mission there."

"Yes, he was," Fran states, wiping away a tear. "Okay, enough of that," Fran says, leaning back against Sam's shoulder as the program starts.

An hour later, Sam returns to the den to get the printed articles. "Ah, it ran out of paper." He looks for more. "Fran," he howlers."

"Yes," Fran replies. "What is it?"

"Where do you keep the paper?"

"It's in the bottom drawer." She tells him as she enters the room, and bends over to look. "Well, I guess Meredith has been busy with her writing assignments. How much are you missing?"

"About twenty-five pages or more. Oh well, guess I'll visit the library tomorrow." He writes down the file names. "Ready? Let's go home." Fran locks the house as Sam carries the laundry to the back set of the car.

On returning to the cabin, Fran says, "So, you had a Winnebago. Did you travel with it every summer?"

Sam starts. "No, we didn't. It was like that four-wheeler a friend enticed me to get so we could race each other or see who could climb the hill the fastest without tipping over. What a waste of money that was! I think it was used maybe four times in the five years I had it. And now, well, I'm thoroughly satisfied with the cabin in the woods."

"What kept you from using it?"

"I was busy with my work. My friend was busy with his work, and Angelia didn't like it from the beginning comparing it to toddlers getting their first Tonka toy truck. That money I spent on those 'toys' would have benefited a wounded veteran."

"You never served in the military. Why not?"

"The draft years were over. At times as I look back, I missed a great opportunity. Dennis, my assistant, had. He enlisted and served three years with the army, trained as a Morse Code operator, spending two and a half years in Germany, and loved it. He got down to Switzerland and spent several hours in East Berlin."

"Yes, "Fran says. "There are times in my life that I wished I could get a do-over."

"Like what?" Sam asks.

"That'll be none of your business," Fran quickly answers. "Well, here we are." She reaches for his hand. "So, my dear, let's make the best of our lives from now on, so in ten years, we don't wish we'd done something different together. Okay? Agree? Promise me, right."

"Yes, sounds good. We're home," Sam says. He takes the dry laundry into the cabin, and as he lights the Coleman lantern, he tells Fran, "I need to fill the tank above the commode, and then I'll boost up the fireplace while you read up on how to play chess."

"Chess? I'm gonna boost you, and I won't regret it." She says with a big smile.

Eight

Ah, this being Monday, and since Fran's at the office all day, I could do some fishing, Nope. It's snowing. His mind wanders as he pours himself a cup of coffee and takes it and a banana to the desk. Looking at the empty typewriter, he mutters, *Not now, maybe later after the library and lunch with Fran.* Sam gets comfortable on the couch, sipping the coffee after a bite of the banana. King comes in from the cold breezy day, shaking the fresh snow off, and jumps on the couch next to Sam.

"Oh, you're cold," Sam tells the dog. He takes the blanket off the back of the couch to wipe and dry his pet. "Now, lie down here and keep me company. I've got some reading to do." Sam opens a history book by Josephus and begins to read. After minutes of reading and dozing, he sets the book down next to King. "Yuck, enough of that." He yawns. *Okay*. He sits at the desk, inserts a piece of paper behind the roller, and stretches his fingers.

My Cabin Life 25

Some things are running in circles around my head, so I must type them out before they get lost. So here goes.

The historian Josephus wrote in the fourth century. Imagine that. A guy, writing pages after pages of history without the use of computer spell-check. No typewriter. No sheets of paper. No ball-point pens or pencils. No dictionaries, only the use of a quill pen on papyrus. He recorded what he considered important information that the next generation should know. Now here we are 1700 years later, and we still have his writings available.

Those people back then in the middle ages, the time of Jesus, and before that, were just as we are in these modern days of easy does it. Our bodies are the same, we walk and talk the same way, we reason and think the same, we form families, and our methods of conversing are the same. They needed to eat and rest just as we do. Writing for them was a chore according to our way of keyboard typing. Our standards of clothing our bodies sure is different than those of four thousand years ago.

Culture determines much as society changes. Sixty or seventy years ago, it was standard for boys to wear suits and ties to dress up for church. The dresses or skirts girls wore to school had to be below the knees, and boys had to wear button-down shirts tucked into the slacks. We cleaned and polished our one pair of nice shoes. Sandals were only for the beach if we had a pair. We followed the standards of the day. Society determines much of what we should or need to do, and it takes time for that new idea to get accepted as the norm.

Where did those kids of two to four thousand years ago go the school? Did they bounce balls, play marbles, skip rope, or ride a sheep or goat? No bikes back then.

We get along or not, and they got along or not in the same ways: yelling back and forth, fights, wars, or letting our disagreements pass so that we can live side by side peacefully. They learned the same way by trying this and that and correcting mistakes. How many mistakes did they make as they were building the pyramids?

Oh yes, people need to relax too, so the rulers announced. "Come to the stadium, watch them fight, and you can cheer while making noise." Was it really a lion? "It's time to have some fun people, so come on out."

I often wondered why it took some six-thousand years to find the secret to electricity. When about two thousand years ago, they learned how to build that approximately three-thousand-mile-long walkable wall in China up, down, and around the hills. Noah learned how to construct that big ship. Wow, would we ever attempt to build a pyramid? The pyramid was put together using something like six-foot-long by three-foot-high limestone rocks on top of each other to form an upright triangle some 480 feet high. Mortar, moistened mud was used to keep them from sliding. The square base is some 750 feet long. History says that it took them twenty years to do it.

How tall was the Tower of Babel? When they built the Empire State building, did they intend to reach into the heavens? That Eifel tower in France points to the heavens above. Skyscraper is what we call our towers. Hmm? Up that high wanting to scrape the sky?

Ha! We can't or won't build a protective wall across our southern border. What's the difference? Was it just a King telling the working slaves to get it done, or else?

Now, we are told by the Washinton leaders what we must do, or else. And the builders must get a permit that meets the bureaucrats' approval after all the methods, material, and design features have been studied and analyzed, and possibly the okay by the people next door. Is it safe and convenient? Who owns the land?

The cost? Will the city, the community benefit? Tax increases? "Yes! Yes! Okay, do it."

Enough of that rambling. I do that too much. But anyway. Now to the present.

Fran asked how I did laundry. Oh, but now we can take our dirty clothes to her home. It sure makes it easier. "Ha," I said, but she insisted I relate the details. For the first month or so, it was a task like many others that made me wonder why I had accepted the offer to move here. I could use it as a weekend getaway. I could rent it out to vacationers. But I stayed and learned much from grandma's notes.

So here goes.

The task of laundry.

First, I pumped, pushing the pump handle up and down many times to get the cold water from the well into the big five-gallon bucket, and then pour about half in another pot to warm on the wood-burning stove, the other half in the sink. When that was hot enough, I dumped it into the sink to warm the cold water. I then pumped another five gallons to warm as I washed the clothes in the sink. I would pull the plug and let that dirty soapy water drain outside.

Then pump more water and use it to remove the soapy dirty scum left on the sides of the sink. Then, when the next five gallons of water on the stove is warm enough, I'd fill the sink and rinse each item, squeeze and twist, squeeze and twist. Put that item on the table and squeeze and twist the next. On and on it went until I could take them all outside to hang on the line to dry. And hopefully, it would not rain.

Whoopie, half the day is gone. Now what?

"King, let's go." Sam grabs his notebook and the USB disk containing the information he needs to print and heads to the library. Reaching the highway, the truck he bought starts to turn into his road. "Whoa!"

Mr.Gambell howlers out his open window, "Sam, Here's your new truck, so turn around and get it."

Sam circles and drives his old pickup behind Mr. Gambell back to the cabin. "Oh, what timing," Sam says. "I was on my way to the library."

"Sam, I could bring it at another time if this inconveniences you."

"No, no, not at all," Sam replies. Let's do it. Thanks."

"It's ready. All the information you need is in the glove box. The title, and the first six-months insurance policy all paid for. Thanks again. Sam, drive me back to town, and it's yours. I believe you'll enjoy it greatly on that trip of yours. Now one more favor."

"What?" Sam says. "I owe you a favor or four."

"When you learn of someone needing a better vehicle, send them to me. No, this is my last transaction, so send them to my son or grandson. I'm heading south for the winter."

"I sure will."

"Here's the key. Now please, drive me home. And, If you decide to do away with that old pickup, the company would gladly sell it for you. I'll contact you later in spring to arrange a fishing time for my grandson."

After dropping Mr. Gambrell off, Sam and King, riding in the back, head to the library in his 2020 GMC truck. *Fran's going to love this. It will be super good for our trip back to Indianapolis.*

At the library, he puts his portable disk into one of the computers to print what he wants. As the printer starts, the laundromat lady, Joyce, greets him. "Hi, Sam. Did you enjoy those nice warm beaches there in Galveston?"

Sam stands. "Hi Joyce, how's things? Those folks down there were wonderful. The beaches, fishing, everything. We didn't want to leave. How's Jack? Haven't seen him since we got back."

"Just messing around. Got another toy to play with."

"A toy?"

"Yeah, since we didn't get to Florida, he got bored. He's been spending a lot of time in the shed tinkering with that thing to improve and make it go farther and faster than those you'll find in the hobby stores."

"What kind of thing? Farther and faster? Is it a drone he's working on?"

"I think that's what he called it. Oh, he's been monkeying around with that since Christmas. He says we're going to be rich."

"Would he mind if I visited him in the shop?"

"No, no! No! Don't come. That's all he's been doing lately. Won't even come in for dinner. I've had to knock on the door to remind him it's past midnight and time to get to bed."

Sam looks at his watch and says, "Oh, I've got to go. I'm meeting Fran for lunch. Joyce, I've enjoyed the chat, and please tell Jack to call me sometime. I'd love to talk with him, ah, perhaps about Galveston. I think you two would love that instead of Florida."

"Sure. Nice to see you again, and tell Fran hello for me," Joyce tells him as he takes the pages from the printer and leaves. Halfway to Fran's office, Sam shouts. "Thank You, Lord."

He parks the GMC, toots the horn several times, and then goes inside. "Good morning," Sam tells the receptionist.

"Sam, Doctor Francinea … Hmm, ha," She says."I should forget the formalities. Fran will be out soon enough. How was the honeymoon? Galveston is a beautiful area. Frank and I had the privilege of going there a couple of years ago. He caught a giant speckled trout. The beaches are fabulous. I think we'll do it again later this fall."

Her phone rings, she puts on the earphones, and Sam sits in the waiting room.

A minute or two later, Fran comes out. "Let's go," She says, greeting him with a hug and kiss.

"I'm gonna drive our new car."

"Huh? How did you know Mr. Gambrell brought it?"

"Oh, honey, you ought to know that word travels fast in this town."

"Hmm? Did you hear that I had diarrhea this morning?".

"No, did you …Oh, I'll give you diarrhea to be so proud of, you'll shout it out to Joanna. Let's go!" Sam gives her the keys, and off they go.

"Where you going?" Sam asks as she starts driving through the winding roads of a neighborhood.

"I just want to experience the comfort of it."

Fran turns out of the neighborhood and onto the main road to the diner.

In the diner, as Joanna escorts them to a booth by the window. Sam asks, "How's everything here? We haven't seen you in a while."

"So, what's it gonna be today?" Joanna asks. "I know, coffee for you and hot chocolate for Fran," she says, giving them the day's menu specials and leaves.

"Well," Sam says to Fran, "How do you like the truck?"

"It's great. Thank you. I love it. Joanna is still struggling with the Sunday closing, so let's pray for her."

They do. During the meal, Sam begins to inform Fran about meeting Joyce in the library but is interrupted. They skipped the desert as Fran had to get back to the office.

In the car, Fran asks, "What did you begin to tell me about Joyce?"

Sam tells Fran, "When I had just finished printing the articles, Joyce Ripper came over, and she informed me that Jack had been busy in his shop tinkering with a drone that he thinks will make him rich. He might have been the one messing around with it over the cabin. I sure hope he calls, and we can talk about it together."

"Amazing. Why don't you go see Jack in his shop?"

"Oh," Sam replies. "She said Jack told her he has to keep it secret until he can get a patent. Then, I wondered if Jack could be the one that solves that drone mystery. After I left the library, these thoughts came to me. If you had enough paper, I would not have needed to go to the library where I met Joyce to learn more about the drone mystery. She was there looking for a book, and I was there to use the computer. The thought came, and I shouted out the window, Thank You, Lord!"

"That was some coincidence, her being there at the same time," Fran says.

"Coincidence?" Sam replies. "I guess we could call it that, but behind the scenes, I believe it was a supernatural working of our Father God arranging our circumstances of when, how, and where we go during the day."

Fran parks the truck at her office. "Honey, I've got an afternoon shift at the hospital and want to drive this there. I'll drop you off at the cabin and see you later."

"Well, ah, okay, I guess," Sam replies.

"Just okay? You guess?" she says. "You got a problem with me driving this?"

"No, no, go ahead. Bring us a dinner back."

After lighting some candles, firing up the fireplace and the kitchen stove, and putting the book back on the shelf, He chooses to read Will Durant's volume One centered on Our Oriental Heritage as he gets comfortable next to King on the couch in front of the fireplace.

Nine

"Hey, Sam," Fran says as she enters the cabin carrying a sack. *Oh, he's napping again.* King jumps off the couch, barking at Fran, and trots to greet her.

"Oh, you're home," Sam softly says. He stands and stretches his arms, and goes to welcome her home. "Anything else in the car?"

"No, hon, this is it. Dinner's from the hospital again." She opens the sack for Sam to see the two meals.

"Guess who I got to treat. Jack was brought to the EMC. He had hurt his fingers and burnt a few spots on his chin, cheeks, nose, and forehead. He told us a project he was working on had unsuspectingly exploded. The worst was his fingers. His fingers looked like a sharp object cut into the tips of his forefingers and thumbs, almost severing them. But we were able to stitch them together. We'll monitor him for possible infection. Whatever he was doing, he won't be doing that anymore."

"Wow," Sam says. "How long will he be in the hospital? Did you ask him what specifically he was doing, and why did it explode"

"Not that way, no. He just said it was a project he had been doing. As doctors, we work to treat the wounds first. The facial burns needed cool water packs, lotion, and bandages. The chin area was the worst and may leave a scar."

"Everything else is okay?"

"Yes."

"When could I see him?"

"In two days, most likely," Fran replies. "After the sedative wears off and the antibiotics get to work. I'll let you know. Now, let's eat. I'm worn out." Fran sets the two dinners on the butcher-block table.

"Besides taking a nap, what did you do?" She asks.

"Was reading Will Durant for a while and then opened that journal to read some of what I wrote when I first got here."

"Why that?"

"I don't know. I guess I got bored with the detailed history Durant prescribed. Rereading what I wrote in the past brings back memories. Like today, a passage in my journal brought back the memory of when I opened my eyes after you stitched up my leg to see you holding my hand and looking at me with those beautiful, compassionate eyes. I think that's when I fell in love with you."

"Oh, that's so sweet. I love you too." Fran leans into Sam and plants a kiss.

"You've read them all, haven't you?" Sam asks her.

"Yes, I have. But I don't recall anything like that in those first journal entries."

"You're right. It was something else I wrote that brought back that memory. Anyway, I pray that you and I never have a problem losing our memories. It's so sad to know or see someone who can't remember their kids and can't recognize them. They're just existing. The body is alive, but the brain has stopped."

Sam then prays, "Thank you, Lord, for protecting us from that. Please do. And, for all those experiencing memory loss, help them recover from that trauma. Why do we suffer like that anyway? Is it because of something they've done in the past? Why? Did Adam and Noah lose their memories in their nine hundredth year before they died, or is this a new problem for us in these technology days?"

"Thank you," Fran says. "Now, let's eat. You got a choice. Fried chicken wings or baked salmon? Got deserts too. Better than cooking on that wood stove of yours, wouldn't you agree?"

"Flip a coin. They both look delicious. Thanks." Sam takes the Salmon.

"Anything else happen this afternoon?" Fran asks as she cuts the chicken.

"Nope. A nice quiet afternoon. Oh, reading some of Will Durant. Imagine that one guy and his wife recording history in seven volumes. Probably five to six hundred pages in each book. Starting with what he labeled as Our Oriental Heritage. In the early 1900s, he attended several universities, became a college instructor, married a student, and traveled the world to gather information for his history series. In those foreign countries, how did he communicate with the locals? How long did he and his wife stay in the countries of Africa, China, or across Europe, and wherever else they went.? What kind of help did he get, and from whom?

"Knowing the technology we have available today and how easy it is to gather information through the internet, I often wonder how they acquired all those details of past generations. Of course, Durant had it easier and quicker than those in biblical days as he wrote all his stuff in the '50s. Without a computer, just a typewriter like the one I have. It baffles my mind when I think about how they accomplished so much, and then I thank God for our blessings.

"It's so physically easy now, and maybe that's part of the reason so many people get diabetic, putting on extra pounds. Yeah, did people get overweight in those days of yesteryear? Oh, that's a subject we don't like talking about. I'm glad I desired to design homes, even though I do like reading history, but in bits and pieces."

"Sam," Fran says. "Why do you do this so much?"

"Do what?"

"Well, like just now. I asked a simple question, expecting a quick answer, but you keep going on and on, rambling away."

'Okay," Sam replies. "You'd like me to shut up." He moves his forefinger across his lips.

"Hon, I'm sorry. I had a stressful day, and I only wanted to relax quietly. Maybe watch a movie."

"Sure. Fine. Let's relax on the couch. You find a movie on that laptop, and we'll watch it together. I'll take care of the dishes in the morning."

Sam blows out some of the candles and gets comfortable in front of the fireplace with his arm around Fran's shoulder as she begins searching for a movie. "Is this one okay," she asks.

"Sure, it ought to put me to sleep."

"If you start snoring, I'm going home. Yes, I think I will." She gets up from the couch. "I need the rest."

"No, don't go!" Sam says, grabbing her arm as she starts to put her coat on.

"Let go!" She insists. "Sorry, Sam."

"What did I do?" Sam asks.

"Nothing! Now let go of me. I'm going." Fran opens the door, gets in the new truck, and takes off as King runs alongside barking and barking.

Standing on the deck watching her leave, Sam ponders what just happened.

Ten

The following day, Sam nibbles down the banana and slurps the orange juice while the coffee perks. He checks the ice box. *Oh well.* He steps outside onto the porch to look at the temperature gauge. *Yes, nice day.* He goes inside to bundle up, gets a thermos full of coffee, and in the barn, he gathers up his fishing gear. At the pier, he tests the thickness of the ice and slowly steps onto the lake.

Some thirty feet out on the snow-covered frozen lake, he removes the snow and chops a hole in the thick ice. Sitting on his camp chair, he drops the fishing line in the water and leans back, thinking about what happened last night. It's a beautiful day, clear blue sky and a warming temperature just above freezing.

What did I say to make Fran so upset that she quickly left and returned to her house? After catching some fish this morning, I must see her and get this straightened out.

An hour or so later, Sam had reeled in five trout, returned to the cabin, and put the fish in the ice box. He cleans the horse's stall in the barn and puts fresh hay in the basket. Finishing the barn work, he exits the barn and hears a vehicle approaching. He hopes it's Fran coming to apologize. Nope, it's the new sheriff. King is jumping and barking at him as he parks in front of the cabin.

"King!" Sam shouts. "Come here! Now! Stay!" King sits next to Sam as the driver's side door slowly opens. "It's okay, sheriff, as long as you don't try to arrest me."

The sheriff slowly gets out of his vehicle. "Good morning, Mr. Guardyall. My name is Frank Goodfellow. I suppose you know that I am Sheriff Olsens' replacement."

"Well, good morning, sheriff. Yes, I do. So, how's things around the county?" Sam turns to King, "Lie down!"

"That's a beautiful dog, but I was never fully trained about these dogs except to be ready to shoot if they run at me."

"King's a good obedient one I trained myself. He likes to bring me a rabbit, and once, he led me to a deer.

"You don't mind if I call you Samuel, do you? I've heard you are living this ancient lifestyle out here all by yourself. So, I should come and meet you."

"Yes, I'm it. And it sure is different than before, but I've adjusted. Would you like to come in where it's a bit warmer? I got a pot of coffee staying warm on the stove."

"Sure, thanks."

Sam and King lead the sheriff into the cabin when King slops some water and takes a few bites of food as Sam hands the sheriff a cup of coffee. "We can sit here at the table or on the couch by the fireplace."

"It's your home. I'm impressed." The sheriff says as Sam leads him to the couch. "I've never seen the insides of a log cabin before. It's intriguing. That bookcase looks handmade, and I assume that's your bedroom behind the curtain. The sink in front of the window next to the stove is great. I didn't notice an outhouse as I drove up. What do you do about that?"

"My grandfather added to the cabin before the area was declared a national forest. There is a restroom and closet behind the bookcase wall. And over there," Sam points to the curtain. "is a closet where my grandmother stored her canned goodies."

"How about water?"

"My water comes from about a hundred-foot-deep well. You know, pump and pump away, and then water comes. Keeps my arm in shape."

Folks around town told me your grandfather built this in the late 1800's."

"My great grandfather."

"And you moved here almost a year ago, right?"

"Just about," Sam replies. *So what's this guy got up his sleeve, asking me all these questions?*

They chat back and forth for several minutes as the sheriff keeps asking Sam more about his life in the cabin, his daily life, and how he likes this small-town atmosphere compared to life in Indiana.

"How was Sheriff Olsen? I've heard that he was like a family member to everyone. Did you like him?"

"Yes, of course, he was like a brother to me. I never thought about him like that, but he liked to go fishing with me. I caught four trout this morning. Do you like fishing? Or, maybe you'd like to walk around the area. One of my favorite spots is next to a stream feeding the lake. That gazebo is a great place to watch nature or a beautiful sun setting over those mountain tops. And to the west, there's a trail next to the national forest, a neat place to take a walk. King found a deer that had been shot, lying in those woods. Yes, it was during hunting season. King also got skunked once in those woods. Back home, I never did any hunting, and I haven't here either, even though my grandfather left a few of his rifles and handguns for me. Do you want to see them? I have a license for that, for fishing, and one to drive my truck. Anything else? How about a little walk in these woods of mine? Want to do that now? It's warming up out there. God has been so great to me in directing my life to this ancient cabin without electricity and this wonderful town. I love it here, and The Great I Am, the Lord of it all, found me a beautiful lady. We were married on New Year's Day. How about you, sheriff? Are you a Christian?"

"Samuel, I just came by to get acquainted. But now I've got to go." He gets up from the couch, puts his jacket on, and opens the door. "Good to meet you, Samuel. Now take care, and if you need help, give us a call." He starts to leave as King runs and barks alongside the vehicle. The sheriff stops, rolls down the window, honks his horn, and hollers to Sam.

"King! Stop!" Sam whistles. "Whew, glad that's over," Sam tells the air as King approaches.

Hmm? Never been in a log cabin before. Where's he from? New York? Chicago? The name Goodfellow? Is he? Oh. I should have asked him about that drone. He might have known something.

Back in the cabin, Sam looks at the clock on the wall. *Ooo, I gotta go.* "King, let's go," he tells the dog as he rubs the neck and shoulders. Sam opens the barn door to get his truck and backs it out. With King on the passenger seat, letting it warm, Sam picks his phone out of his shirt pocket and calls Fran. Ring, ring, ring, *Is she in the office or at the hospital? I forgot. Ah, she must be busy.* Sam sets the phone on the dashboard and starts to drive to her office. The phone rings as he passes the town square.

"Sam, honey. Sorry I missed your call." Fran says. "I was interviewing a patient. I'm at the hospital today. How are you?'

"I'm okay. Did some fisting this morning. Oh, not a boxing match. Fishing for fish. Then the new sheriff dropped in to introduce himself. Oh, I didn't mean drop in, like, ah. Oh, forget that. He stopped by, came to watch, to see, to ….." Sam forces a cough. "Ugg."

"Sam, you're not making sense. What's going on?"

"I don't know what happened there. Fran, are you okay? Did you get a good night's rest?"

"Yes, I did, thanks to you. I'm sorry about the way I acted last night. I know I was kind of brutal to walk away from you so quick. Forgive me."

"Yes, of course. I'm here at the office now. Can I bring you anything?"

"No, I'm fine. Got that meeting this afternoon with the superintendent, so I'll know more then. Right now, I got another patient to check on. Hey, let's have those fish you caught for dinner tonight. I'll bring the onion rings you like. See you at the normal time. I love you, Sam. Bye."

"Thank you, Lord." *Okay. That's over. Now why the heck did I get so confused? Is this a sign of my mind blocking out? Whatever those specialists say is a sign of dementia? Am I going crazy or just getting old? Yuck, this can't be. I'm only fifty-six.*

On the way back to his cabin, Sam starts singing one of his favorites. "When peace like a river, attendeth the way. When sorrows like sea billows roll. It is well with my soul. It is well. It is well!" Arriving home, he sees the ice truck and Norman coming out of the cabin.

"Ah, just in time. Thanks. King, you remember Norman here, right?"

"Woof, woof." King barks and sits next to Sam after getting rubs by Norman.

"Mr. Guardyall," Norman says. "You got a new ten-pounder." He pauses, looking down. "Dad told me that if you're here, he wanted me to tell you about the rumor going around that you shot down a drone."

"What? I shot down a drone?"

"Yes, that's what I heard."

"From who?"

"Some guys from the, I think it was fish and wildlife, as I've seen that same truck. Three days ago, I heard two guys talking about it in front of the library while I was putting trash in the dumpster. Did you shoot one?"

'No, I did not. I did see one while I was on the lake fishing. So, I've been wondering who was managing that thing. All I've been doing is asking folks around town. Did you get a good view of them?"

"They were standing behind that black truck. Like ah, watching folks going in or out of the library and asking them about you."

"Me?"

"Yes. They called me over as I went back inside and asked me if I knew you."

"I said yes, I deliver ice to you. That's all."

"You say it was a big black truck? Any symbols on it? Were they wearing uniforms?"

"Just black jackets. The license plate was white with big blue numbers."

"That means the truck was registered out of state, not Colorado. Do you think it could be a Federal vehicle?"

"It could be."

"Umm. Thanks, Norman. I heard the scouts are having races with drones, right?"

"Yes, we do. Oh, it's been terrific. Over the big playground, we strung circles, squares, and triangles that we must fly through in a certain amount of time. Come on out and watch. We'll be doing it again in two weeks this Saturday. Starts at one-thirty, right after lunch. Well, time for another delivery, or dad will be upset. See ya."

"Tell your dad thanks. I appreciate it."

Sam watches Norman drive away as King runs, kicking up snow alongside the ice truck.

"King, I need to take a walk. Perhaps sit by the stream." Sam follows King toward the lake. Sam turns left near the pier and throws a tennis ball out toward the trees. King brings it to Sam, drops it, and backs a few steps, looking up at Sam, waiting for another toss. Back and forth they go until they reach the stream. Sam unfolds the camp chair and reclines, giving King rubs. After several minutes of quietly letting his mind wander, focusing on the wilderness, the lake, the blue sky, and the snowy mountains. King barks a few times and takes off upstream and into the woods.

Oh, he saw something. Was it a rabbit? I could follow his steps, but no, I'm here to relax.

"Oh, Lord. How did you do it?" Sam speaks into the air. "It's amazing when I think about it. Thank You for these quiet times." He raises his arms and starts singing, but then King returns, swagging his tail back and forth and barking at Sam while taking a few quick steps toward the forest and back to Sam barking again. "No, I don't want to," Sam tells the dog. "No, King. Sit!" King barks again, waving his tail. "Yes, buddy, I know that look, but not now." King then takes off, runs about five steps, stops, barks back at Sam, and then backs up a bit while continuing the woofs.

This better be good. Sam gets up and follows the dog prints in the snow alongside the stream. He nears a turn to the left when he sees King wagging his tail. "What is it?" Sam says. A step away, Sam sees a bloody mess. He takes a more concentrated view seeing what appears to be the face of an owl. "Hmm?" *Was it shot? This is not hunting season. Who would want to kill an Owl?* Sam looks around the area, between the trees, and starts walking further upstream. King leads the way through the dense forest and soon comes upon the pond the beavers had put together. Suddenly, Sam stops. *Well, I'll be.* Right there, lying on the frozen pond is a drone. He picks it up, and turns it over when one of its wings is hanging by a wire. He walks back to the spot they found the owl and covers it with snow. Sam carries the broken drone back to the cabin and sets it on the table. He carefully examines it. *No bullet holes in this, so it wasn't shot down.*

Could it have crashed into the owl? But I don't see any blood. Oh well. So, whose drone is this? Is this the one I'm accused of shooting?

Sam hears a knock on the door.

"Well, hello there." Sam declares. "Come on in."

"Hi Sam," Susan greets. "Peter wanted to show you his album and tell you the news."

"Yes, Peter. You did it. That's great." Sam says. "Yes, I've been wondering if you've continued that hobby."

Susan tells Sam that he and two other students were chosen by National Geographic as student trainees on a trip to Israel to see, witness, and take pictures of the many rivers, lakes, and places like the Dead Sea, the Sea of Galilee, and other bodies of water."

"Wow!" Sam says as he shakes Peter's hand and pulls him in for a hug. "That's fantastic. Congratulations. When you going?"

"Leaving on the fifteenth," Peter answers.

"Will you accompany him?" Sam asks Susan.

"No," She replies. "They said they will have a teacher along to continue schooling since it's a two-month trip. And, of course, I'll be able to see it all through Youtube."

"Oh, Peter, I'm so proud of you. But how did they find you, out here in rural Colorado, and discover your interest in photography?"

Peter replies, "I was in the library one day and saw an advertisement requesting local pictures of rural areas around the country. Some kind of a contest. So I did."

Susan adds. "We got a call a month later. Then a visit, and well, here we are."

"The other students? Do you know where they're from?

"The man from the company," Susan says. "told us they are also from rural areas. One from Arkansas, and the other from Idaho."

"Oh," Sam says. "Thank you, Lord. Now watch over Peter, and guide him, protect him on this extraordinary trip. Your ways and means are beyond our imaginations in guiding Peter to respond to an ad."

"Thank you, Sam. You've been a blessing to us since that first day," Susan says.

Peter says, "Mr. Guardyall, do you mind if I take a few shots of this?" Peter asks, looking at the drone lying there on the table.

"No, I don't. Yes, YES, do it." Sam agrees. "And, could you print them for me?"

"Sure. They'll be small, three by five,"

"Wonderful. Thanks, Peter. And, Susan, thank you for bringing Peter today. The timing was fantastic." While Peter is snapping the camera, Sam looks the album over to see the fantastic pictures taken over the past few years. Peter dated each one but let the viewer interpret what the photo portrays. "Susan, would you mind periodically updating me on this trip of his?"

"I will, Sam. Oh, we're so proud of him. At first, it irritated us that he was spending so much time with the camera you gave him. We thought it'd be better as a family to relax and watch a movie together or even go to a Rockies game. But then his dad saw the gift developing and gave him the latest type of camera for his birthday in August."

"Yes," Sam says, "He does have that God-directed gift."

Eleven

"O, Fran, how good it is to see you. How did the day go? I missed you." Sam pulls her in for a hug and kiss.

"Very good," Fran replies. "Sorry again for my action last night, but I was tormented by the thought of the superintendent's meeting. The rest and quietness at the house helped. But still, I shouldn't have left so abruptly. Forgive me."

"Yes, of course. I love you, and that's over and done. Oh, I had a dream last night. Wow. But how did that meeting go?"

"I got a minor promotion to patient wellness after surgery leading up to the patient's dismissal. I will ensure the patient is psychologically ready to return to normal life. And it comes with a raise in pay."

"Sounds like it's right up your alley, as you've been doing that all along. So, they finally discovered your talent in that area."

"But the downside is that I'll be on-call. Anytime, day or night."

"Will you still be able to vacation away for two weeks this Easter?"

"I asked him about that, and he said yes. But then he added an if."

"An if what?"

"He couldn't explain. Well, you know how we suddenly get surprised at times overloading and disrupting our services. We'll have to wait and see. Now tell me about that dream of yours."

"I've been typing it out, but let's eat first, as the fish is ready."

"Oh, I forgot the onion rings. Sorry."

"Hey, that's ok. I fried some mushrooms. It's all ready."

They consume the fish and some split peas at the butcher block table. "So, Sam, what else did you do today? The weather is warming. This afternoon it was a high of thirty-eight, so soon enough, you'll be able to take the boat out."

"You were here last year," Sam says. "How quickly did the lakes thaw then?"

"Don't recall," Fran answers. "Sometime in late March, so we have another month for spring to arrive."

Sam says. "Hmm! Did the people back four, five, or eight hundred years ago discuss the weather when they sat on the floor eating fish? When did temperature gauges become part of our lives?"

"Temperature gauges?" Fran responds. "Not anymore. We check the cell phone or the TV to get the forecast."

"Since moving here," Sam says. "I've been wondering what life was like in those long-gone days. That first week or so without a cell phone or computer, days would roll past, and I may not have known what day of the week it was until I got into town. I bought a calendar and started marking days off as I climbed into bed. Yeah. Now I've got you to keep me up-to-date. So, tomorrow is Tuesday, or is it Wednesday?"

"You know what tomorrow is. On your calendar, you have Monday the twenty-sixth crossed out. As a little girl, mom would tell me what day it was. She had a big blackboard to write our daily chores and notes on. She'd put a line through it or erase it after her inspection. If I did my chores, then I'd get dessert after supper. Whoops. Now we call that dinner time."

"Yeah," Sam says. "When did supper become dinner?"

"Who cares? Now, come on, tell me about that dream you had."

"Oh," Sam says. "That may take a while. I'm still thinking about it. But ah, let's finish, ah . . . din-supp, clean the dishes, and then get comfortable on the couch. Okay? And, remind me to get a blackboard, so I can write your chores on it."

"Yes, get one. A big one: I'll write your chores down every morning before leaving for work or before bedtime. Get red chalk too."

"Red chalk?"

"Sure. Use to imply its importance over the others. If it's not done properly, no dinner for you."

"Ah, good. Then I can lay in bed watching you fiddling with that antique wood stove to cook your dinner."

"Woof, woof, woof," King barks at something he sees out the window. King goes through the doggie door. Fran settles in on the couch, watching Sam add more wood to the fireplace.

Sam reclines next to Fran. She carefully puts the blanket over their shoulders and opens the laptop to find a movie. "This couch was left here by your grandparents, right? Or did you get a new one? It looks and feels like new."

"One of Grandpa's notes indicated he bought this several months after Grandma passed. Comphy, isn't it?"

"Yes, it is," Fran says. "You know that the first time I heard about this cabin, I wondered if everything inside was as old as the cabin itself. It intrigued me, and I wanted to see it myself. It wasn't too long, and I did, when Harry and Meredith talked me into going with them to remove the snow off your driveway."

"That was a big surprise when you all showed up. Seeing you and having that snowball fight was a turning point for me. Until then, I had no desire for another wife or even a date. King removed the loneliness. I was so engaged in adapting to this life without electricity that things outside became less important. How do I say it? I knew what society required but didn't know what cabin life required. Yes, it was a struggle to keep focused. But God guided me one day at a time. Sitting by the stream became a favorite spot. Watching the birds, the squirrels and rabbits, and those beautiful white clouds looking like cotton balls dancing through the air. Yes, God led me beside these still waters. Back in Indianapolis, I had no idea that a quiet voice told me what to do or not to do. Couldn't hear it. Too busy for that.

Work had to be done. Gotta get up at six. Gotta finish that design. Don't forget this or that. Want to watch the Cubs tonight. The Colts? The bills are building up. Cancel that. A new meeting. Grass must be cut, and weeds picked. Find a different way to do it faster. No, I don't need that. On and on it went. Church? Well, I guess we ought to go."

Sam leans forward and turns his head to look at her eyes. *Oh, she fell asleep.* Sam leans his head back and closes his eyes.

A few minutes later, King enters through his door and comes next to the couch, twisting his cold, damp hair.

"Woof, woof," King barks at Sam.

"Oh, what is it?" Sam says as Fran wakes up. "King, stop it. Lie down," he tells the dog touching its nose.

"I guess I took a nap," Fan says.

'Yes, we both did," Sam says as he looks at the clock next to the fireplace.

"How long was I under?" she asks.

"Maybe half an hour or so. It felt good. Fran, it's only seven-ten and too early to climb into bed, so what now?" He adds two logs to the fireplace, then rubs her shoulders, "More hot tea?" as he takes a few steps to the big table to refresh the chilled coffee. Fran rises from the couch and joins him.

"What now?" Sam asks, handing her the cup of hot tea.

"Let's play a game. Monopoly?" she suggests.

"No. How about chess?" Sam says.

"No. on second thought, I'd rather watch a movie. Movies are more relaxing. Grab my laptop, and we'll snuggle up on the couch."

Two hours later, the movie ends. "That was interesting. Can you imagine yourself under those circumstances?" Fran asks.

"No way!" Sam answers. "Near the end, I realized that was the last movie Angelia and I watched together two weeks before she went home to her eternal mansion. I just had a thought. Do you think that your Jerome and my Angelia know each other up there?" He points to the sky. "Can they visualize us here on the earth? Why not? That is a spiritual world out there. And here we are in the physical realm. Our time is not yet. There's more for us to do, and what is that?"

"Honey, there's nothing more for tonight, so I'm going to bathe and go to bed. Come on."

"You go ahead," Sam says, "I'd like to finish writing about that dream. It shouldn't take too long."

Sam sits at the desk and starts to read the note he started several hours ago.

My Cabin Life 25

I very seldom dream, and if I do, It's usually gone when I wake up, but I had a dream last night that's hard to forget.

I was building a home, a place to live where the rains would not penetrate the insides. I was puzzled by how to keep the rain from leaking between two tree trunks. I was putting some kind of putty, black in color, between the wood. Should I put a small branch inside the putty?

And then this.

I was walking thru the aisles of a Wal-Mart. I stopped and looked up and down this one aisle, scanning the shelves. Thousands of items. I started to wonder how each item was packaged. Some in cans, some in plastic or cardboard. How was the packaging done and sealed? Where? How did it get to the shelves of the store. Where was it shipped from, and how long did that take? What processes were used for packaging the item. Where did it come from? The cover described what was inside, and someplace on the package were these black perpendicular lines. What was that? Why was that there? Who created the inside product?

I next saw tables with many different fruits and vegetables. Where did they all come from? They had to be grown somewhere. How did the farmer determine the best time to pick and package them to be shipped to a distribution place and then to stores? What stores? Where and why those?

I saw hundreds of books. How did it become a book? Where and how was the paper made, and what kind of a process was that? The typewritten pages, the binding. How was it put together? The black and colored ink had to be processed, packaged, and shipped. Same with the binding glue. Inside there was a note indicating it was copyrighted. Huh? How and what was that process? Why?

He finishes reading the previous entry, leans back, and closes his eyes to bring the dream back into remembrance. He begins again.

That was it. I woke up. I took a break and sat on the porch, and these thoughts came. All of these processes developed over a couple of hundred or so years. Then, I wondered how humans a thousand years ago lived their daily lives without the technology we have available today. How did they contact those in the family tree to celebrate a birthday? Birthday cakes? Candles?

If they wanted ketchup, where did they get it? Salt? Pepper? What did they do if they got a headache? Did the kiddies have kindergarten? A pet dog to play throw and fetch? Books to read? Calendars to keep track of appointments? Clothes to wash in the stream or lake? Soap? Combs to brush their hair? Bathing suit to wear when jumping off the diving board.

Oh, no pool in the backyard. No riding mower to keep the grass short.

"Well, that didn't take long." He mumbles, seeing Fran in her pj's crawling under the covers. He blows out the candles and the lantern and slides in next to her.

Twelve.

"Honey," Sam says to Fran as they slowly consume break-fast. "I made a decision last night while watching that movie. That drone I've been pestering folks about. Let the drone be a drone, and whoever is operating that thing can do what they do with it. It will not bother me anymore. Done and over with. Let it come."

"Why? Didn't you consider it an invasion of your privacy?"

"Yes, I did, and it is, but so what. I don't do anything illegal. The one thing the drones cannot invade is my mind and soul and whatever I or we do inside this cabin. It can watch me fish, feed the horse, my walks with King, leave the area, and watch me return. And soon, I'll prepare the garden and perhaps have the scouts in for a weekend campout. I don't own the air above this property, so I surmise it's free to use it. I don't care. And, yes,

I hope the guy using that drone enjoys all that humdrum stuff and perhaps learns something about remote life.

"And, come to think about it. Our Father God is also watching us and knows our thoughts. But God surveys us for our safety, guiding us in everything we do, think, listen, and obey. Now that's love."

"Oh, Sam, you've got a knack for understanding it all. I love the way you do it."

"Another change. I've enjoyed writing my cabin life notes, so soon, I will start to write a novel about escaping from society to live in a log cabin during these tumultuous times when technology directs everything we do. Well, not me, as living in this cabin is outside of technology, and I love it."

Fran starts, "Sam, I think I understand what you're saying. You're used to this cabin life, and I'm not . . . yet. I'm working on it, but it'll take time. Getting more comfortable with the daily tasks took you some time." Fran pauses.

"Well, it's Tuesday morning, and it's time for me to get to the office."

As she gets in the car, she reminds Sam to get the blackboard and chalk while you're in town for lunch. "See ya then, twelve-thirty. Bye."

Back inside, Sam refreshes his coffee and sits at the desk. He flexes his fingers as he prepares to start typing on that old Remington. Okay, here goes more thoughts to put on paper about those scientists telling us how, when, and what all this is about. Why? According to them, there is no Why. It just is.

My Cabin Life 26

Oh, we have it so easy here in the twenty-first century.

Our scientists tell us that all this came to be over billions or trillion of years by atoms and molecules bumping and merging together. Da, da, da, da, they postulate. All that started with a big bang, they say. Hmmm? Can nothing go bang?

Those tiny atoms we can't see supposedly randomly merged to form everything there is now. From the moon, stars, our sun, and for us, eyes to see, a brain to interpret and remember, a beating heart, lungs to breathe, bones and muscles, hard teeth, and a soft tongue. How did those atoms form tiny soft hairs in our ears, hard toenails, fingernails, and soft, thin skin holding all of the above together? Wow, and it only took billions or trillions of years of bouncing around to do that.

How about life, the ability to move, to breathe in and exhale on our own?

The God Almighty created light to pierce the darkness by saying: "Let there be light." And it was. Stars, moon, the earth Ball with fresh and salty water forming clouds, rain, and lightning storms. Then, this Almighty created the birds, the big eagles, and on down to hummingbirds, flies, and mosquitoes. Oh, the elephants, tigers, horses, dogs and cats, and the various water swimming creatures. All three animal groups breathe and move according to their designed DNA.

Every one of these land and sea creatures burst with life with the built-in ability to see with eyes, to hear with ears and a mouth to eat, and also the ability to reproduce, and then, yes, us two-legged humans with the additional capability to imagine, create, and love. Then with our first disobedience, we added hate.

The ancient people, way back, used that innate ability to imagine and create. Yes, they built the Pyramids, that wall in China, and boats for deep water fishing and for crossing the oceans. They constructed Stonehedge, Castles, and Colosseums. Made blankets, clothes, ropes, swords, and pottery to drink from and cook in.

They survived for thousands of years without the stuff we take for granted. But why not light bulbs? Surely, the ancients experienced lightning storms. Did they not wonder what that is, how it works, or what causes it? Is there something here that attracts something in the clouded sky?

Here I am, wondering what the ancients did, as we have it all, even space ships to land on the moon. Telescopes and microscopes to see out there or in here.

And we still can't get along. It's like the sign I used to have hanging on the wall of my Architectural company: "*the* Captain is always right. And I am the Captain."

Oh, that's it for now.

Sam pushes himself away from the desk after removing the last page of his notes and files them in the folder labeled 'My Cabin Life' notes.

"Where's King?" Sam opens the door and briefly looks around the area. 'Hmm?" He closes the door and goes to his closet. Coming out dressed for the cold weather, he slides into his boots and grabs his whistle. Standing on the porch, he blows it several times. "Ah, here he comes," Sam says as King runs out of the barn.

"Whatcha been doing? Keeping the horse company?"

"Woof, woof." Sam turns and follows King through the beaten-down snow tracks to the barn. Upon entering, Sam sees that Wonder, the horse, is nibbling on hay. King jumps up on the stack of three high hay bales with his nose pointing up. "Woof."

"What's up there?" Sam asks. He looks into the rafters, and at one end, he sees two eyes looking down at him. "Ah, a kittie cat up there. King, you want a cat to play with?" Sam gets the ladder and places the top near the beam the cat is lying on. He ascends the ladder. In a high-pitched voice, he softly says, "Kitty, kitty, kitty, meow, meow." He holds his hand out, but the little kitty backs up. "Oh, there's two of them," he notes as another cat moves a bit. Sam continues to persuade the cats but to no avail. Leaving the kitties alone up there, he descends, leaving the ladder there.

"Come on, King, they found a way up there and will find a way down." King follows Sam out and closes the barn's door so that King won't disturb the cats anymore.

Sam gets the key to the truck, signals King onto the passenger seat, and off they go to town. *Where do I find blackboards?* He stops at the Ace Hardware store to get a couple of gas refills for the Coleman stove and lantern. "You don't have any blackboards here, do you?" he asks the clerk.

"Yeah, sure we do. The makings of them. Easy enough to do. What size? Hey, you're Mr. Guardyall, right? You may not remember me, but I was at your scout camp last spring."

"Ah, I guess not. Your name is?"

"I'm a Samuel too, like you, but my friends say, hey dude."

"Shouldn't you be in school now?"

"I quit. Now, I home-school till August, when I go to Brigham Young in Salt Lake, Utah. They've accepted me to play golf."

"Are you Mormon?"

"Not yet, but I guess I will be."

Sam replies. "Wow, I come in here to check on blackboards and discover you. Samuel Dude, you've got quite an adventure ahead of you. I wish you well. God surprises us daily, and I'm sure you'll discover one surprise after another in your search. That's a wonderful educational school over there. Have you picked a major field of study?"

"Archaeology and Anthropology."

"Huh? I'm not sure I understand the connection between those."

The dude replies, "I don't either right now, but why society develops like it does is intriguing. I shouldn't be spending all this time about that stuff. Let me help you get your supplies. What size board do you want?"

"Two by four, I suppose. That ought to be big enough."

Sam is led through several areas where Dude helps him pick the supplies; the smooth plywood, primer, rollers, and black enamel paint, and briefly tells Sam how to do it.

"Nah, I don't need to frame it." He also selects several colors of chalk, white, red, green, and yellow, plus two erasers. "Hey, Dude, thank you so much. I'll try to remember you in my prayers. Good luck."

He puts it all behind the pickup seats. And heads to Fran's office. *I can put that together this afternoon, and Fran will discover it this evening hanging next to the door. I'll divide it into two sections: one for each of us, and also, an area for supplies needed, and on top, the verse of the day.*

"Good Afternoon, Sam," Fran says as she sees him waiting in the office. "Where to for lunch?"

"Ah, let's go see what Joanna has for us." Sam escorts Fran to the new GMC truck as King jumps off the old pickup bed and jumps into the back seat of their new truck. Sam opens the rear window for King.

"Did you get the blackboard?" Fran asks as he backs out of the parking spot.

"Well, not exactly, but you'll see it this evening when you get home."

"What do you mean not exactly?"

"You'll find out later," Sam replies.

"Oh, another suspense game you're playing, eh?"

"I got it all at the Ace store, and the clerk who helped me was at a Scout camp last spring. He's got a golf scholarship to Brigham Young. Good kid, he'll do well." Sam parks the truck along the sidewalk by the diner and escorts Fran inside, where Joanna quickly seats them at Sam's favorite booth next to the window.

"Haven't seen you two for a week or so. Whatcha been doing?" Joanna asks as she places the daily menu in front of each.

"Sam replies, "sleeping, working, eating, and of course, talking."

"That seems unusual for you, especially the working part. The special today is fried fish with mushrooms but no onion rings. I'll get your coffee and tea when I get around to it," she says and leaves the booth. As she leaves, Sam loudly says, "So you're the one who's been spying on me with that drone."

Joanna stops, turns back, and says, "I don't have a drone, but I do have two ears." And she walks away.

"Now, honey. Let's not irritate her. She's still having trouble accepting the diner's closing on Sundays," Fran tells him.

"But hey, think about it. We had fish and mushrooms last night, and here we are, and she suggested we have the same here. Sounds fishy to me. And that part of no onion rings. Is this really one of those coincidences?"

"Hush. Stop it."

Sam gets quiet, looks down at the menu, reads the entrees, and starts to twiddle his fingers. He glances out the window at the cars driving by, some folks entering and leaving the courthouse. His eyes peer at the grey clouds under the white ones.

"Think we'll get more snow this week?" he asks Fran.

"Possible."

"Somethings are always possible, except eighty-degree weather tomorrow. Oh, that'd be nice, wouldn't it?"

Joanna and another lady approached the booth. "This is What's up," Joanna says. "Meet our new waitress, Luwana. She has a speech disability, but she hears very well." Luwana nods her head and sets the coffee and tea down while Joanna asks what it'll be for this late lunch.

Fran says she'll have number three, and I think Sam will have the same, except he wants those thick onion rings instead of fries.

"Okay," Joanna says as Luwana gives them a thumbs up and nods her head as they leave the booth. Joanna then sits in the booth, leans over, and says, "Sam, you were an architect, right? I would like to have our roof redone. Could you, would you design a church-type roof to replace that ugly flat one we have? Something like those antique churches in Europe. You know, like Notre Dame. And I want it to reach high above the courthouse's roof. And it must have a high cross on top, and I'd like our name, 'café' up there too, with a big underlined sign that states, We don't serve Sundays here."

"What?" Sam replies. "Are you serious? Joanna, when I moved here, I left all my design tools back there. I don't have the necessary tools, so I couldn't do that, even if you were serious. Do you know how much something like that would cost? And, you'd have to get permission from the county, and probably the state to see if it exceeded the height requirements and if the extra weight wouldn't exceed the ground stability too. And also how the flow of rain water, and melting snow might affect the area surrounding the building. Just that process would take a year or possibly more."

"Why, Joanna? What brought this on?"

Fran then says, "Joanna, are you doing this to rebuke your parents and their insistence on closing the diner on Sunday?"

"You don't know how much it has affected us? Yes, I'm upset. I emailed dad the results this past couple of weeks, and he replied that working on Sunday may affect my chance of being accepted into heaven, and I want to see you there. I replied that we, all of us, still go to church at the Wednesday services."

"I understand what you're indicating," Sam says. But, isn't there a more peaceful way of objecting?"

Fran then adds, "Sam, you could use my laptop, or one at the library to sketch it out for Joanna."

"Yes, do it, please, and leave the rest to me," Joanna says.

"I guess I could. But Joanna, this may take me a few days. Are you in a rush?"

"The sooner, the better, as I may have to start doing some cooking myself. So, thank you. I appreciate it, so when you get it, bring it in. I'll be waiting."

Luwana brings the meals to them. Nods her head and gives the dishes a thumbs up. She then points to Sam. She points her two fingers to her eyes and then those two fingers at Sam. She turns and points to a young man sitting at a table toward the back of the diner. She points at the man, then to Sam, back to the young man, she rubs her heart, mouths her lips up and down, and points to the guy, and then points to Sam.

Sam says, "Are you telling me that the young man you pointed to wants to talk to me?"

With a joyful look, she nods her head three times and gives a thumbs up.

Sam says, "when?"

She moves her finger, writing the letter N in the air, closes her hand, draws an O, and draws a W.

"You mean he wants to talk now?"

Again, she smiles and nods her head. She then points to the food dishes, brings her hand to her mouth, then turns and points to the young man and her watch.

"Ok. We'll eat first, then bring him over. Thank You, Luwana. You're very good at sign language. Thank you." Sam says and bows his head.

She bows two times and leaves the booth.

Thirteen

The young man approaches the booth. "Mr. Guardyall, my name is Alexander Summers. The Indianapolis Star sent me to see how you're doing on your adventure. They want pictures of the cabin. They've given me a week. Would you be willing to show me around your cabin? I just arrived this morning. Flew in to Denver, rented a car, and booked a room in that Easy Inn in Johnsonville. I could do it at your convenience."

"Well, Mr. Summers," Sam says.

"Oh, please call me Alex."

"Okay. Alex," Sam replies. "This is a surprise, and I'll have to think it over. If the Star had contacted me previously, it might have saved them the trip's expense. I enjoy my privacy, this small-town atmosphere, and the secluded life in the cabin, and I don't know. I did not move here to become famous. I've come to enjoy the privacy."

Fran interrupts Sam, "Sam, honey, this may have been initiated by my friend Susan in Shelbyville. She indicated her friends and many others desired to know more about you since we were married."

"Well, tough," Sam quickly replies.

"Mr. Summers," Fran says. "Would you mind if Sam and I discuss this later this evening? But now, I've got to get back to my office, and Sam has already scheduled this afternoon. Sam or I could contact you tomorrow."

"Okay. Yes, I'm sure this is a surprise, and I wish the office had already contacted you. It'd make it easier on all of us. Here's my phone number, and I'll be waiting for your call. God bless you both." Alexander gets up and leaves.

In their GMC, Sam scans the parked cars and those readying to see if Alex is driving one of them. "Dang it," Sam declares. "I would have liked to know what kind of car he was driving," He tells Fran as he shifts forward and starts the drive to Frans's office. He continually looks in the mirror at any cars following. He suddenly turns into a neighborhood.

"Where we going," Fran asks.

"Oh, I just wanted to see if that black car was following us," Sam says, taking several deep breaths. "Sorry, Lord."

He turns around at an intersection and drives back to the main street to her office, two blocks away. As they and King exit the GMC, Fran says, "Now honey, don't let this consume your thoughts the rest of the day. Leave it be. God has you. And this evening we'll discuss it more. I'll call Susan this afternoon and see if she knows anything about this."

"Yes," Sam says as he pulls her into a hug and a quick kiss. "Thanks."

On returning to his cabin, Sam turns around and parks near the diner. As he pushes open the door, he looks around and signals to Joanna. He sees that his favorite booth is empty. Joanna comes over and asks, "What you want Sam? This isn't like you. Wasn't the food good?"

"Please sit with me for a few minutes. Can you? I've got a few questions for you."

"Sure, but first, let me notify Luwana." Joanna signals the waitress. When she approaches the booth, Joanna tells her. "Take over, as I'll be here with Sam for a while, but bring Sam his coffee." Luwana bows her head several times, turns, and returns to a table with a family not too far away. "Okay, Sam, what's on your mind."

"Back last year, when I first entered your diner,' Sam starts. "You've impressed me with your hospitality and knowledge of the town and area. I was immediately impressed with your service and the food, and it appeared to me that you cared for every customer. You did that to me. I appreciate it."

"Okay, I get it," Joanna says. "You want to know what I found out about that young man from Indianapolis."

"Well, yes, that's one."

"After I greeted him, I didn't get a chance to ask him anything. He got right to it and asked about you. Said he'd like to meet you. Where was your cabin? What did I know about you? Were you friendly? And more. I stopped him and asked what he wanted to eat, telling him this is a diner, a place to enjoy a meal with friends and family, and I was not his Ouigy board. I took his order and left." Joanna then tells Sam. "Then I saw him sit down and talk with you, and you heard his request, right?"

"Yes, I did," Sam says. "He told me the newspaper in Indianapolis sent him here to interview me, get some pictures of the cabin, and perhaps spend some time with me at the cabin. I was surprised and told him I'd have to think about it. He gave us his phone number to call when I was ready. He said he has a week, so that's still up for God's guidance. Fran and I will discuss it tonight." He sips his coffee, looks at the restaurant's ceiling, and says, "Now, Joanna, on another subject. Your future here in the diner. That design you want to replace the roof. You're not a church. You and others have heard that your father demanded you to close on Sundays. You've done that, and now you've hired some disabled gals as waitresses. So, what's really going on?"

Joanna tells him. "After I told dad of the decrease in business by closing on Sundays and that our waitresses quit as I had to decrease their hours. Dad suggested I hire some disabled waitresses to extend our compassion to those who've had a tough time in life because of an injury or birth defect. That's our Christian duty," he reiterated.

"After thinking about it for a few days. I put an ad in the paper. Luwana was the first, as she was a secretary, was fired after she fell ill with the flu for three months. She answered my ad, and I thought, well, why not? Give her a try. She was excited to return to work and is doing well. And then I heard of Janice with just one leg moving very well in an electric wheelchair. I hired her, and she's doing well too.

"A week or so later, many, including pastor Thomas, have positively complimented me for doing it. And surprisingly, now the business is beginning to increase again.

"Let me pray with you over all this." He reaches across the table for Joannas' hand. He starts praying softly for her direction and desires to extend the roof.

Joanna smiles as Sam finishes his coffee, and he tells Joanna to keep her eyes up and ears open. "Now, I've got to get home to finish a project for Fran. I'm glad I stopped to check on all this. Be brave and keep on keeping on. I will prepare a sketch for you as soon as I can."

"I'll be waiting for it. And let me know how it comes out with the journalist." When Sam rises, he tries to hug Joanna, but she quickly leaves the booth.

Back in the cabin, and after stoking the fireplace and stove, Sam starts assembling the blackboard. He's applying the second coat of enamel paint when his phone rings. He flips open the cell phone and sees it's Fran. "Yes, hello."

"Hey dear, I just got off the phone with Susan, and yes, she knows the journalist and says he's legit. Yes, she contacted the Star, and briefly told them of our getting accustomed to living in a cabin. Mark said that when we come there at Easter, he'll play a round of golf with you. We'll discuss it more this evening. So take care, and I'll see you in an hour or so and bring supper." She hangs up.

Sam finishes painting the blackboard. He dresses for the colder weather, summons King, and they walk the path to his chair by the stream feeding the lake a bit of water running under the frozen lake. King runs off into the woods. After a half-hour of solitary quiet, Sam returns to the cabin to hang the blackboard next to the door. On the blackboard, he divides it with bold white lines.

King enters the cabin through his doggie door. He shakes his wet fur and nibbles a few bites from the bowl, and then Fran comes in carrying two sacks. She's hanging up her coat and notices the blackboard.

"Well, great timing," Sam says.

"Oh, Sam, it looks great. Thank you." She reads the chore Sam wrote under her name. She picks up the black eraser and removes it. "I love it, honey, and the space on top for a scripture. Thanks. Now, let's eat a bite. Joanna fixed us your favorite baked beans and a slab of baked ham."

As they sit at the butcher block table, spread out the food, and after a brief blessing, Fran says, "Joanna told me you stopped and talked with her. Was that about the journalist?"

"Part of it was," Sam replies. "She explained more about the Sunday closings' effect on her restaurant. She's not fighting it anymore, as the two new waitresses, even with their handicaps, have increased business. People are beginning to like it. She said Pastor Thomas complimented her for doing that. Her eyes have opened to the Sunday day of rest that her parents initiated. I'm all for it, too. Opening stores on Sundays started back in the forties and fifties during our industrial revolution. So, now we don't have an official day of rest. That's up to us."

Fran says, "It was interesting to watch Luwana as a waitress and how she communicated with us with those hand signals. Interesting. Now, what about the journalist?"

"I'm beginning to welcome the idea," Sam says. "Would that be okay with you, as he also wants your feelings about the adjustments?"

"I thought about that. Susan said that many of those I used to work with would be interested in reading how I'm doing married to a guy in a log cabin. They can't imagine themselves doing it."

"Hey, thanks for bringing the food," Sam says while he slides the cushioned chair toward Fran. "Now, it's time to stoke the fireplace to warm us up before bedtime."

"Yes, do it. Did you fill the shower tank with warm water?"

"I did."

"Thanks. That's your daily chore. See ya in a bit," Fran tells him as she skips toward the bedroom.

Sam cleans the kitchen and adds the paper plates and napkins to the stove. At the fireplace, he puts three logs on the simmering wood. He watches them start flaming and returns to the kitchen area to add wood to the stove. Sam pours another cup of coffee when the coffee pot is warmed. With the kerosene lamp on the table next to the couch, he gets comfortable and begins a rough sketch of church steeples Joanna wants to add to the diner's roof.

Fran approaches and settles under the blanket beside Sam on the couch. "Oh, that's beautiful. Did you do that just now? Do you want to call Alex now, or you'd rather I call?" Fran asks.

"Yes. No, later."

"What?" She exclaims. "Is it Yes, or no to my calling Alex?"

"Um, you asked two questions. Yes, I just did that sketch, and no, to you calling Alex. I'll call him in the morning."

Fran relaxes comfortably next to him, solemnly peering into the flames rising in the fireplace.

The next morning, after his morning chores in the barn and a brief visit to the dock to test the lake's ice, Sam calls Alex.

"Alex, this is Sam. When would you like to see my cabin?"

"Anytime you're free for a few hours."

"Well, come on down. We could do it now or later. Up to you. Do you know where it is?"

"Yes," he replies. "I got a description of your entrance by the roadside stand. Also, Google Earth it. Great! I'll be on the way shortly. Oh, ah, would you tie up your dog? They terrorize me sending shivers all over. Something from my childhood."

Sam replies. "King's good with people. You'll have no problem from him."

"No, I'm serious. I've got a phobia about big dogs."

"Well, I guess I could put him in the barn while you're here," Sam replies. "Now, he's out running around the woods somewhere. Give me a bit or so to find him. He usually returns for a bite to eat soon. Call me when you get to the fruit stand."

"Thank You, thank you, Sam," Alex says. "I will." And he hangs up.

"Oh, well, "Sam tells the air. *A journalist with a phobia?* Sam dresses for a walk in the woods, gets his whistle, steps out on the porch, and blows it three times. Waits a minute and blows again. He steps off the porch and turns toward the barn. He slides the barn door open, and there is King jumping and running to Sam.

Sam reaches down and rubs his pet's cold ears, his throat, and down between his legs. "How did you get in here?"

"Woof, woof, woof."

"No, we don't have a door number three." Sam looks back at the entrance door that slides on rollers. Sam peers into the first stall, where the hay bales are stacked. The next stall is where his horse is kept. He looks around the barn for any sign of an opening. Sam fluffs up the hay on the floor and rubs his horse's nose up to its ears, back down, and the area between its front legs. Sam takes a few steps to the rear of the barn and the last stall where his firewood is kept, along with garden tools, the roto-tiller, and mower. "Ah, there it is," he says out loud. "Did you do that," he asks, looking down at King. The dog turns his head, pointing his nose up. "Woof."

"Are the kitties still up there?" Sam positions the ladder and climbs to see. No kitties. He grabs a shovel and four pieces of his logs. He lays logs into the dugout entrance, and shovels dirt to fill in the hole, and then adds logs along the entire length of the rear of the barn. He looks at his remedy. *That should do it.* "King, let's go in the cabin for a bit."

As they leave the barn, Sam closes the door, and they step onto the porch. Inside, Sam grabs a blanket, the dog's water, and the food bowl and returns to the barn. "Now, King, You'll be here for a while." He lays the blanket on one of the hay bales, the food, and water on the dirt floor next to the hay. Sam quickly leaves through the doors' narrow opening, quickly shuts the door, and pulls the latch down. He walks around the barn to inspect the filled opening from the outside. Turning the corner, Sam sees a small animal running into the woods. "Oh, you're the one. Was that a possum? Now, you go ahead and dig again. Yeah. Try it."

He looks at his watch and decides to walk to his entrance road to the highway and wait for Alex.

Soon, a black car slowly turns into his road, and it's Alex. He rolls down his window and greets Sam leaning against a post. "Good morning Sam, How are you? Been waiting here long?"

"No, not much," Sam answers, and strolls around the front of the car and gets in the passenger seat next to Alex. "How are you this morning? The sun is beginning to warn us about spring coming. So, ah, you want to see my lifestyle."

"Yes. Thanks."

"Well, This is the starting line I encountered ten months ago. I arrived in Prairieville by bus with my backpack, a duffle bag, my dog, and a picture too. In town, a local guy volunteered to take me here. Otherwise, I'd have had to walk those five miles carrying all that stuff from home."

"Whoa! Not so fast," Alex interrupts. Alex reaches into his shirt pocket to retrieve a small black instrument, pushes a button, and lays the device on his thigh. "You don't mind if I record our conversations, do you?"

"If I said yes, then what?"

"I'd turn it off, get my pencil, a pad, and start writing."

"Would I be able to read your writing?"

"Okay," Alex says. "let me start at the beginning. Using the recorder is easier and will make this visit faster. At the hotel, I'll listen and slowly type it all out. I'll bring you a copy of the document, with the pictures, which I'll send to the Star, with your approval signature. Everything we submit to the publisher must have the interviewee's approval. Sometimes, the editor will call to ensure he/she has seen and approved the document." Alex turns to get his briefcase, pulls a document out, and hands it to

Sam. "This explains it all, Sam. And I'll need your signature here also."

"Thank You," Sam says. "With my business in Shelbyville, we did most of our advertising with the Herald as they seemed to have the greater readership."

"Your architecture business is called Guardyall Designs, right? And you sold it to Dennis when you accepted the offer to occupy this cabin. Dennis said he was amazed at the terms of the sale and couldn't believe you would do that. He's doing great work now. He asked me to tell you how much he appreciated your encouragement in those years when he first started."

"Dennis was, is great. He didn't need encouragement. I did."

"What were the terms, if you don't mind?"

"Easy, like buying a house. A small down payment and then ten percent of the yearly profits. This cabin was free of debt and no utilities to pay each month. I suppose one could say that buying the wood for the fireplace, candles, and oil for lamps could be considered utilities. So, I didn't need the money. The sale of the house, my cars, furniture, and all was plenty. God has blessed me way beyond anything I could imagine. No health issues. A clear mind and body that's been forgiven. And now, just recently, a life companion. Are you a believer, Alex?"

"Yes. My wife and I go to a church in Indianapolis." Alex takes his foot off the brake pedal, and the car slowly moves down the narrow road to the cabin.

"Since my arrival was mid-spring, "Sam begins saying. The birch and maple trees were leafing out, and the pines were great, what I called a canopy to the trail. Oh, do you have your recorder on?"

Alec nods.

"When the car approaches the small curve, Sam says, "Right about here, I had to stop to take in the beauty of it all: the lake and the forest leading up to those snow-topped mountains. I felt like I was looking at the cover of National Geographic. My dog had been running through the woods and caught me here in a daze. Wow! That is all I could say. You'll see the cabin and barn as we go around this bend."

Alex stops, steps out of the car, and snaps several pictures. "It is a beautiful setting, Sam," he says, returning to the car.

"On the right here, that open half-acre is where my grandparents grew vegetables. Grandma left many notes on how, when, and what to plant. On one of her notes, she indicated she always saved some for the church to give away. They sold a bunch at the entrance shack. On the left is the barn where my horse is kept, wood for the fireplace and stove, and garden tools. My dog is locked up inside, so you may hear his barks wanting to get out to greet you."

"Oh, I'd like to, but I've tried different techniques they said would help. I've even thought working alongside a veterinarian would help."

"Hey, that's all right. We all have a deep-seated fear of something. I feared dropping everything and moving here. At first, I was excited and thrilled, and then the reality of living without my computer, cell phone, and all that stuff, like no hot water, no heater or air conditioning, light switches, and fans, hit me hard. We all do some of that on camping vacations. But to live all year long without any of that jolted me. Ain't no way, and I decided to accept the offer and use the cabin for yearly vacations. My secretary told me to stop complaining, take the leap, and get going. It'll work out. She reminded me that God initiated it, and He'll walk you through it. And here I am ten months later."

"Sam, what a story. Now, where should I park the car?"

"Right there in front of the porch."

He does, opens the rear door, and gets a briefcase, a laptop, and a camera bag with additional lenses. "Take me inside, Sam."

"You got a jacket or sweater, as it's cooler in there than in your car."

"I'll be all right."

"Okay," Sam says as they step up onto the porch. "Stop right there, Alex," Sam tells him as he steps in front of Alex. "Not yet. Let's sit in these rocking chairs for a bit to let the atmosphere sink in. I started to do this on my, perhaps on my second, fourth, or tenth day. I'd sit in this chair, and rock back and forth, enjoying what I saw. Okay, now do this. Breathe in deeply. Look at the leaves of the trees. Focus on the little ripples on the lake. Close your eyes and breathe again; hold that breath a bit, and let that fresh air slowly out. Now let your eyes wander around the area as that fresh cool air encompasses you.

"I learned to make this one of the first things in the morning to sit here and do just that. At first, I did it to see the surroundings and enjoy the solemn quietness as I nibbled on a banana and sipped my coffee. And, petting King. Then, as I saw the animals, the birds, the individual trees and forest, the sky, clouds or a clear blue sky, or feel the winds of an approaching storm, or gaze down to the blades of grass, a dandelion here and there. I became mesmerized by it all, struck by the marvelousness of this planet, everything in it, and the God up there, down here, who did it. I'd breathe in again and hold that breath thinking I was breathing in the spirit of God, and I didn't want to let it out." Sam breathes deeply again and says, "Sound foolish?"

"No. The scripture says, be still and know," Alex says.

"One morning, some ants got my total attention. They were crawling from that end of the porch to here and up this post, then under the beam. Yes, under the beam, upside down without falling. They went up the post without slipping and falling backward. How? To get to the string, down the string into a flower shape of the hummingbird feeder to get some of that sweet stuff. Then back down the beam bumping into the ones going up for more to take back to momma. Did they greet each other with a "Hi, Joe. Yes, it's good. See ya, Pete."

He continues. "One morning, my hand got my attention as I was bringing the cup of coffee up for a sip. Two fingers through the cup's handle to hold it, and the next one under the handle. My wrist rotated the cup between my lips to drink the coffee. Wow, what a design! Four fingers, each with three knuckles, attached to a squarish palm. And a shorter thumb, all leading to a rotating wrist. Wow. Amazed I was."

Sam turns to look at the young man beside him, who's looking at his hand. Sam takes a deep breath and says, "Enough of that. Let's go inside."

"I'm beginning to feel what you envisioned," Alex says. "And, guess what, I'm not feeling a chill. Not a bit. The recorder has it all."

They both leave the wood rocking chairs and approach the front door. "Looks like you got a doggie door there, right?" Alex asks.

"Yes, I did that several months ago when winter approached. Now, he can come and go as he wants. Don't be concerned. He's locked up." Sam opens the dutch door for Alex.

"Oh, Sam, I love it." Alex sets up the tripod, attaches the camera, adjusts the lens, and starts the movie process from the right all around the room. "When was this built?" he asks Sam.

"My great-grandfather built this in the mid to late 1800s, after his arrival in 1847 from Norway. According to notes left for me by his son, my grandfather, he completed it in five months. Now, why he settled here, I don't know. There have been some rumors about an Indian tribe that had occupied the entire area and driven away when the Americans started spreading out, as this small area was the only open area around this lake. But that doesn't make sense, either. I didn't think our native Indians cut down forests to settle and put their teepees. I think the forest on our right would have merged with the forest on the left. That's nature. There is a small stream on the western side but nothing but woods on the eastern side, a few yards past the gazebo. The eastern forest would have met the western part up to that stream. Trees cover all of it. So, a bunch of trees had been cut to clear the area for the cabin, the garden, and the approach to the lake. But then I wondered how he removed all those stumps. None of the bulldozers we have now to yank them out. Horses? Of course, he used some of the trees to make the cabin, furniture, that butcher-block table, desk, and the bed frame. But how long did that take? The deed to this property is in the local county courthouse, But still, why he picked this land has not been answered to my satisfaction. He was from Norway, and that's a woody area like this part of Colorado. So, I suppose that's where he…"

"Sam," Alex cuts him off. "You keep going on and on from one subject to another,"

"Oh, sorry, Alex."

"It's all interesting. But would you please just answer my questions? I'm supposed to be the interviewer."

"I do that a lot Alex. You should have been here when twenty some students came to see the cabin. The civics teacher wanted his class to see and learn more about civics from me."

Sam sees the look on Alex, "All right, I'll shut up."

Fourteen

"Sam, when you first stepped inside the cabin," Alex asks, "did you stop in wonder seeing it three-dimensionally? That's a bit different from looking at a picture."

"Oh, yeah," Sam replies. "Like you just did, I stopped, frozen in my steps. But then King rushed around the room, smelling everything and jumping up and down on the bed. That brought me back to reality. I dropped the sack and yelled at my dog. Then I looked around. I was amazed at the stone fireplace and its beautiful construction of various-sized rocks and stones strategically placed. Wow! Being an architect, I was amazed at the workmanship. I ran my fingers over some, and then the reality hit as my fingertips left marks in the dust."

"It was chilly in here, too, right?" Alex interrupts.

"Yes, it was a bit. That was in the first part of April, so it wasn't too bad. Grandpa had provided for a friend to add wood to the fireplace daily over the winter to keep the insides from freezing."

"Now, Sam, I'd like to describe what I see around the cabin step by step. It all will be recorded. Along the way, I may ask you a question here and there, but please, do not interrupt."

"Okay, I'll go take a nap on the couch. When you describe me, I'd like to hear that."

Alex has his camera, and the microphone hung around his neck ready as he turns toward the kitchen area.

"This is the kitchen," he speaks into the mike. "A handmade red cedar butcher block table, three by five, with four strong homemade chairs."

Alex continues describing what it feels like, what he imagines it may be like to prepare a meal baked in the antique wood-fired belly-shaped stove. On and on he goes as he takes pictures of everything from various angles. He describes the closet, the bookcase, and some titles and starts to describe the bedroom, "well, not really a room," he says, "as the bed area is open, except for a curtain to close it off." He describes the addition Sam's grandfather made when he was able to connect to a dumpster for the shower, toilet, and sink water. "Before that, they had an outhouse." The refurbishing removed five feet from the main living area of the twenty-by-thirty-foot cabin. In building that wall, he left the top open for heat from the fireplace to settle in there. Alex snaps pictures of the hand-made desk with the Remington typewriter, a half-dozen shots of the stone fireplace, and the stack of wood. Standing several feet away, he gets a few shots of the couch facing the fireplace.

"I'm finished here and now want to tour the outsides."

"Go ahead," Sam says.

"Come along with me. Show me your favorite resting place."

"Just follow my footpath to the left. I think I need to check on the horse and King. It's been several hours, and they both may need water and food."

"Okay, I'll follow you."

Alex is closely behind Sam as he opens the barn door. King runs and jumps on Sam. "King, sit! Sit!" Sam commands. Looking at Alex backing away, King barks a few times at him. Sam bends over and rubs the dog's ears and down his neck.

"Alex," Sam says. "King was saying hello. He'd like to shake your hand."

"Ah," Alex, a few steps behind Sam and the dog, he timidly says, "ah, okay."

Sam, holding King's collar, guides the dog closer to Alex. "Now, Alex, bend your knees."

"King, sit and shake hands with Alex." Sitting on the snow, King raises his right paw up in front of Alex, and Alex slowly lowers his right hand to hold the dog's paw. "There, now you're friends." A bright smile overcomes Alex, and he then carefully touches King's nose and rubs his neck. Seeing King enjoy the rubs, Alex kneels and starts to rub more and more as King raises his head, licking Alex, and pushes him over onto the snowy ground. "Woof, woof," King barks and licks Alex more as the dog lies on Alex's chest to get more rubs. Alex raises his arm in front of the wet tongue as he rolls to his left and right, trying to avoid those wet slimy licks.

"King! Stop!" Sam grabs the collar and pulls him off Alex, who stands, reaches back to brush the snow away, and checks his camera and recorder.

"That was recorded!" Alex shouts. "Wow! Sam, here," he hands the camera to Sam and shows what button to push for the movie. "I got to have some more of King and me. My wife would love to see this."

"Okay, What?"

"If I stand here and call King, will he come and shake hands with me?"

"Sure. I'll have King sit next to me. You clap your hands, get down on your knees, and he'll come. The rest is up to you."

Alex backs up. "Sam, I'd like to have the barn in the background, so stand over there."

"Gotcha."

Sam records it all for the next few minutes of Alex's play time with King.

"Oh, wow," Alex replies after viewing it. He pulls out his cell phone, presses a few buttons, and tells Sam, "There, I had to. Couldn't help not letting her see it. Oh, Sam, you've… I don't know what to say… I'm . . . oh, so thankful."

"I see that," Sam says. "God has done another miracle in your life, Alex. He did it for you as you followed along, cooperated."

For the next half-hour, Alex tours the area, taking pictures of the gazebo area, and the scene there. He stands on the pier getting shots from the left to the far right, where the lake's mountain stream feeds the lake. Along with Alex is King, following him. Alex throws a snowball for King to catch and runs back, shaking his snowy hair at him.

"Oh, Mr. Guardyall, Sam, I thank you so much for this opportunity, and foremost in my mind has been overcoming my fear of large dogs. Thank You. Thank You!

"After seeing the movie of King and me playing together, my wife texted me back, asking if you'd let us visit you sometime this summer."

"Of course. I'd like to meet her. She sounds like a beautiful, wonderful wife. You are blessed with her, and God has blessed you this day, and don't forget it. Goodbye and safe travels," Sam tells him as he gets into his car.

"Bye, Sam. I'll send you a copy to approve before it's posted."

King barks and runs alongside the car and out of sight. Sam returns inside to warm up. He refreshes his coffee and sits staring into the fireplace.

King comes in through the doggie dog, laps up some water, and bites some food, then jumps on the couch next to Sam. "Hi, buddy. Cold out there?" King lies with his head in Sam's lap, getting those rubs. Relaxing with his head back on the couch's pillow, Sam concentrates on the warmth of the fireplace.

An hour or so later, Fran enters the cabin waking up the dog. King's barks and his sudden moves to greet Fran wakes up Sam. "Well, Hi," Sam replies to Fran's greeting as she removes her boots.

"That's all I get is a hi?" Fran replies.

"Come over here, and I'll greet you properly," Sam tells her.

She dons her wool robe, joins Sam on the couch, leans into him, and gets a long compassionate kiss from Sam.

"Hmm! I think I'll return outside, and we can do this again." Fran says, leaning her head against his shoulder.

"So, how did it go with Alex?"

"Take a guess."

"You enjoyed showing him what and how you've been living here in this old cabin. Am I right?"

"Partially, yes."

"Oh, playing hide and seek an answer, are you?"

"Sure, why not? That's your job as a physician, to discover the ailments that harm people. You should be able to discover what I'm hiding from you."

Fram pushes her elbow into Sam's side, straightens up, and peers into his eyes. "Oh, I'm gonna discover and treat your ailment right quick. You're sleeping out here on the couch tonight."

"Oh, good. I'll be warmer next to the fireplace."

"Not without the blanket," Fran exclaims as she stands and pulls on the blanket covering the couch. Sam grabs his end, stands, and pulls her closer and into his arms, and they both fall back onto the couch, chuckling.

As they're relaxed on the couch, looking at the wood burning in the fireplace, Sam describes to Fran how Alex lost his fear of large dogs and then texted his wife a movie of him playing with King. "After that, he was a different guy and wanted to know if he and his wife could visit sometime this summer. Overall, it was a good visit. I behaved, kept myself from rattling off, and let him describe the cabin into his recorder. He'll bring me a copy of the visit for approval before publication."

"Great. Now I'm ready for a snack or dessert of something," Fran softly says.

"Dessert? We haven't eaten dinner yet. Whatcha bring us?"

"Nothing?"

"Well, then a dessert will do. I sure would like one of those cinnamon apple pies you're so famous for. I know that's out of the question tonight. A scoop of ice cream? Will that do it along with a chocolate cookie?"

"Surprise me. I'm tired."

After quickly enjoying the chocolate cake with a scoop of vanilla ice cream, they both lean back, staring at the flames rising in the fireplace. Then a nap.

Sam leaves Fran on the couch and slides onto the chair at the desk.

My Cabin Life 27

Oh, this visit with Alex got me thinking of the first few days, weeks here. Yes, it was beautiful. But adjusting to this primitive nature, I wondered if I had done the right thing. I missed Angelia. She would have been helping me adjust or demanding to return home. Nice for a weekend in summer, but all year long? It was hard. I made it through the first week by the grace of God. Then I came upon some notes Grandpa had left. Reading those of his and also some of Grandma's notes settled me down, and I made that vow: I will do it. If they did, I can. And, I will too.

Now Alex is a new man as he lost that ingrained fear of large dogs. Yes, where and how do these fears encompass us? Why? The Bible tells us to fear not, for He, the Almighty God is with us. Do not fear! But we still do. Well, all I can conclude is that we're here in this physical body, and we like it. We like to walk around and smell the roses, and we don't want anything to disturb that daily life. We protect our bodies. But we're also subject to our surroundings, our society.

Just now, I surmised what it might have been like for our soldiers fighting off the enemy. They're in trenches, and the commander yells, "Go." And they rise out of the trench, knowing that perhaps the enemy may start firing at them. They run toward them, and perhaps on the way, they see a comrade or two falling to the ground, but they keep obeying the commander, who is running alongside or behind a bit, yelling, "go, go, go." Are the troops fearing for their lives? No, I don't think so. They're committed to obeying the commander. They've got to, or else, later on, they'll be imprisoned for not obeying.

Now, why don't we think like that when we submit to and let fear of something overtake us? Is that not disobeying God?

Fear is just an emotion, right? And our emotions change rather quickly sometimes, just as it did with Alex. He knew his fear was irrational. He told me so, but he still let that fear of large dogs overtake him. Now he's free. And I suppose my hesitation in allowing him to document my life in this cabin was a fear of how other folks would react by reading about my life.

Anyway, it's over and done with. Alex is happy, and I am too. Alex learned, and I did too.

Fifteen

Sam finishes reading the story Mary suggested he read to the kindergarten kids sitting in a half-circle on the library floor facing him while she's away attending to an emergency.

"Do you know what that word 'violet' in the story means?" Sam asks. They put their coloring books down.

A boy raises his hand and quickly says, "That's like a big lion. Another student interrupts the first, saying, "No, It's a bird, don't you remember what the teacher showed us?"

"No, it's a color, a girl says.

"It's not a color." A boy says. "there are only three colors, like that flag."

"No," another girl adds. "Look at our crayons. A whole bunch of colors."

Sam then says, "in the story I read, it mentioned a flower."

"Yes, a flower," A girl says.

"Okay, okay, kids. Quiet down. Maybe you'd like to ask me a question."

"Yes," a girl raises her hand. "You look like my grandfather. How old are you?"

Sam tells her, "I'm fifty-four. Now, how old are you?"

"I had my five-candle party last week."

Their teacher walks into the room with a bag, and the seven kids rise and happily scramble to her, embracing her legs. "No! Now sit down. I've got something for you."

"Yeah, yeah," they holler.

She sets the grocery bag on a chair and hands each student a bag with a red bow tied atop the green paper bag. "Okay. One -two -three, open it."

They tear into the bags throwing the paper on the floor, finding a candy bar and a handful of popcorn. Some open the candy, and some put popcorn in their mouth.

"How's it been for you, Sam? Thank you so much for doing this."

"Is your husband okay?"

"Yes, he's doing well. Just a badly bruised arm. Nothing broken. He's on the way home now. Have they behaved? I'm sorry to leave them with you."

"That's all right. I'm glad I was available. God is always teaching me something. Yes, Mary, the kids were fun, and they may have learned something from me."

"Yeah? Good. I was hoping they would. What was that?" Mary asks.

"That I'm fifty-four," he says, smiling.

Mary chuckles at that and faces the kids enjoying the goodies. Some are throwing popcorn at each other. "Stop it!" she yells. "Now pick it up and put it in the can over there. Now!" Standing at attention, her arms across her stomach, she patiently watches the kids until the floor is cleaned of their mess. "Okay, good! Now line up. It's time to go." The kids line up single file, the shortest one first. "Now, say thank you and goodbye to Mister Sam." They do and follow Mary out of the room, out the library door and get on the bus.

Sam, watching them leave, says, "No more of that, Lord. Please!" He gets into his truck, exits the library parking lot, and stops at the diner.

"Afternoon, Sam. You're kinda early today." Joanna says as he reclines in his favorite booth. "What's up?"

"The ceiling."

"One of these days, that ceiling will be lower," Joanna replies.

"That is the plan. The construction will start next Saturday evening at about eight. Since you've agreed to a simpler renovation, we've got the go-ahead. They will work at it all day Sunday and should finish later that night so that you can re-open Monday morning. Are you okay with that? I was at the library using Skype to chat with Ralph, and he briefed me on it."

Joanna says, "Ralph was here a few days ago and told me. We're closing earlier Saturday to give us time to remove our tables and chairs. Thanks. Dad and Mom are coming and will be available to help."

"No rain is forecast," Sam relates.

Joanna signals Luwana, who sets a cup of coffee in front of Sam.

"Thanks, Luwana. Is Joanna treating you right?"

She smiles, points her hand toward Joanna, and then brings her free hand to touch her heart as she leaves the booth. Sam asks Joanna, "where's Janice?"

"Ah, she quit full-time last week. Too much for her. She wanted to work but couldn't handle five days straight. We've got an opening. Are you ready? You can start tomorrow."

"Ha! That'll be the day. There was a Down Syndrome teen-age-boy working at the library you might be interested in."

"Sam, I've got work to do. Thank you for all you've done in designing this addition. Don't forget your meeting with dad and mom on Saturday at eleven." Joanna leaves and enters the kitchen.

Sam finishes his coffee, gets in his truck, and returns to his cabin. He opens the barn door to check on the horse. King comes running out of the woods. "Whatcha been doing?" Sam asks as he rubs the dog's neck and jaw.

"Woof, woof, woof." King watches Sam fill the water bowl, adds some fresh hay to the stall, and rubs his horse's neck, ears, and nose.

"No kitties up there today? Did you find a rabbit? Come, let's go warm up in the cabin." Sam closes the barn door and walks to the cabin, following King. After he hangs his leather jacket on the hook, he adds wood to the fireplace and the pot-bellied stove. He pumps water into the coffee pot to heat. Adds some food to King's bowl and freshens the water. *This used to be a chore, but it's now second nature.* He notices some papers on the desk, along with the book by Josephus. He takes the book and his coffee and gets comfortable on the couch facing the fireplace. After lighting the lamp, he opens to the bookmarked page and reads more about Solomom. Several minutes later, his cell phone rings.

"Oh, that must be Fran." Sam gets up and looks for the phone. *Where did I put it?* He struts over to his jacket hanging on the hook and removes the phone from the pocket. "Hey, Fran."

"Sam, this is Wanda."

"Wanda! Oh, it's good to hear your voice again. How's things going? Did you have a great Christmas and New Years? I've been thinking about you and Dennis."

"Yes, we did. But now we've got a problem. Dennis is in the hospital. Been there for a week now. He's got pneumonia and more. They don't expect him to be able to leave for another week and then possibly go to a rehab center for another two to three weeks. He may pull out of it or may not. Kacky is doing the best he can to finish the New Comers Flat, but he's falling way behind. And Aboman just up and left and took some draw-ings with him."

"What? Oh, my," Sam says. "But Dennis will recover, right? And what happened with ah, Aboman? You said he took some drawings? Why would he do that?"

"Oh, he began fussing with Dennis for a few months or more about his work, feeling like he wasn't getting the pay he deserved. Sam, Dennis promised the company everything would be ready in two weeks, and now all that detailed work is gone, and Dennis is sick, we won't make it. Kacky's been working on it day and night, but still."

"That's a crime to remove and take a company's swork. You've notified the police?"

"Yes, we did, but they can't find him. Without those papers, we're stuck. We won't be able to keep our contract."

"Wanda, I'm so sorry. Were they not saved to the computer?"

"He took the thumb drive also. Sam, I hesitated to call you and ask for your help. But we … is there any way you could come and help? I'm terrified the company won't survive if we don't meet the deadline."

"Oh, Wanda. I don't know." Sam bows his head. *God, help them, and me too. Guide me. I promised Joanna to discuss her project with her mom and dad. And Fran too, needs me to guide Meredith with her drawings for the school project. I can't leave Fran alone.*

"I know this is sudden, but we need you," Wanda declares. "I've already checked the Denver flight schedule, and one is leaving in the morning at five after eight to Detroit. Then a transfer to Indianapolis at ten-thirty will get here at eleven-ten. I could pick you up, or you could rent a car. There's another flight to Cincinnati, but it leaves earlier at six-forty."

"What's the name of the company, and the one who's overseeing this project?"

"Building Times Go Right is the company. Headquarters in New York. Norman Abrams is handling it."

"New York?" Sam scribbles down the names. "Wanda, I'll call you back in a few hours. I know you've prayed about this already, and I have too. Can Dennis receive calls?"

"Yes, he can. He's at St. Peters. Room 402."

"Oaky. I'll let you know in a few hours. Bye, Wanda."

Oh, Lord, You've heard this and know what's happening. I ask for your help and guidance. And for Wanda too. Please Lord. The company must survive. What should I do next? I thank You for having finished Joanna's project. Fran will need help while I'm gone. Meredith too. And the men's Bible study at church. Ah, Lord, you know my schedule and promises better than I do, so guide me. Open the doors that need opening. Let me hear your Spirit. Thank You. Oh, and lead the police to where Paul has gone. You know where he went. Now lead the police to him and get those drawings returned. Amen.

"Fran," Sam says when she picks up her phone. "A big problem at the company has erupted, and I believe I must go there to help. Leaving in the morning. I may be gone for a couple of weeks."

"Sam, dear. What happened?"

"I'll tell you more this evening. Right now, I've got phone calls to make. Just wanted you to know first. See ya later."

"Sam, Sam…"

Sam rushes out of the cabin to his truck. "No, King! Stay here." On the way to the library, thoughts cross his mind. *Now, why didn't I get phone numbers for the New York office, the name of the contractor, and the project? Oh, she told me. New Comers Flat. And Norman Abrams. But is it in town or Indian-apolis? What kind of a project?*

At the library, Sam researches for information. He calls the hospital for Dennis, who couldn't talk then. He makes several calls to the New York office of Building Times Go Right. He talks with Norman a bit and tries again to connect with Dennis. He talks to Wanda again and to Kacky. He calls Dennis again and connected and talked with him for several minutes, bringing

Sam up-to-date on the project. Back to computer searches for another half-hour. He's been taking notes of his calls and search material and printing them to take home. He's back in his truck and stops to see Joanna to cancel his appointment with her parents. He stops at the church to cancel his appearance at the Bible study group.

"Pastor Thomas, I may have to leave this evening to catch a flight early in the morning." He checks with the vet about caring for King while he's gone. Sam then returns to his cabin and starts packing his suitcase. *It's almost five-thirty, and Fran should be here soon. Oh, I don't want to leave her here alone. Maybe she would stay with Meredith. And Harry might be able to help with the horse, and King too?*

Sam's phone rings.

"Yes, Pastor Thomas," he answers quickly

"Sam, I called Gene, and he has offered to drive you to Denver."

"But, what about his classes?"

"Sam, it's spring break. Let him know when you want to leave."

"Oh, thanks. Thank you. Thank you. "

"God is directing this and all the details too." The pastor says. "Take a moment to relax and give thanks. You're blessed, and we'll miss you at the Bible studies. We'll be praying for you."

Fran enters the cabin, "Sam, I brought us dinner."

"Oh, I'm so glad you're here. We got so much to discuss, and thanks for the food. Let's enjoy 'em here by the fireplace."

"Come and get it."

In a few minutes, they're comfortable on the couch. "My turn to pray," Fran announces. After her short blessings on the food and Sam's new dilemma, she asks, "You said you'd be gone a couple of weeks. Is that definite, or could it extend beyond that?"

"At this point, I don't know. How do you feel about this?"

"It's what you must do. I understand. I've already talked to Meredith and will stay with her. I can take King. He'll be able to run around the fenced-in yard. You'll be able to call from your office there, and we can have our online chats. I'll be fine, but I'll miss you. Where will you stay? A motel?"

"Wanda and her husband have two extra bedrooms, as their kids have moved out."

Sam takes a deep breath, relaxing in the warmth of the fireplace and the blanket. He wraps his arm around Fran, pulling her close. "Thank You so much for understanding. You're my love, and I'll miss you. Now, I need to turn in. Gene is picking me up at four. The flight from Denver leaves at six-forty."

Sixteen

Sam rushes through the door to his previous architectural company. "Wanda, I'm here."

She runs over to greet and hug him. "Thank you, thank you. Oh, Sam, you look so fit and handsome. You've lost some weight, too. How's that married life?"

Kacky comes trotting down the stairs. "Sam, just in time. Wanda got us sandwiches, fries, and cheesecakes for lunch."

The three sit around the lounge table, chatting and catching up on Sam's new life in the cabin. Sam explains how it was at first, how he adjusted to life without any modern conveniences. He briefs them about his recent marriage, the honeymoon, and the quaint small town.

Wanda asks, "Knowing what you know now after a year of this, would you do it again? How is Francinea adjusting to cabin life?"

"Yes, definitely, I would," Sam replies.

Kacky rises. "Remember when you chided Dennis and me? Don't just sit there. We need your help. We got work to do. So take over. There, I'm giving it back to you."

"Yeah," Sam tells him. "Good one. Wanda, any news on Aboman?"

"Nothing new. He's gone. No trace whatsoever."

"Want some good news? On the flight here, I remembered something. Back ten years ago, when computers became common, in addition to saving our work on the thumb drive, I set it up to automatically save everything to Wanda's computer's cloud drive. Since we never had a problem with the thumb drives, Dennis and I forgot about that safety save. It should be there."

"Wow! Sam, you're a genius. If they're there, you just saved us a bunch of work."

Wanda quickly sits at her desk and points to a folder as Sam and Kacky watch. A few minutes later, she hollers out. "We got it!" Kacky jumps up and around in circles. "Yah ha! Now I can go home and rest a bit from these ten to twelve-hour days."

"Well, good. Thank you, Lord. Now let's go get a steak to celebrate."

"We can't leave. Norman Abrams is coming over soon. He wants to check how's it developing."

"Well, good," Sam says. "Kacky, let's go up and see what you got. Wanda, print those lost drawings and bring them up." They ascend the stairs to the large drafting room.

"Wow!" Sam exclaims. "You guys have done a great job of updating the area. "Amazing."

"It was Aboman's idea."

"No kidding? How was he anyway? Was he a good draftsman?"

"He was, Sam. Really! I felt like a wannabe next to him. His imagination, putting those ideas on paper, and creating 3-D models were impressive and greatly helped us. Over there is a Lego-type model he put together."

"Then what was the problem that caused him to leave abruptly?"

Wanda interjects, "I believe Dennis was intimidated by his work. They always argued and fussed over using Dennis's design or Abomans. Dennis did not want to go the way of the Frank Loyd Wright Modern look."

"Wright? Would the owners we're working for want that?"

"No, they did not."

"His problem was that he didn't respect Dennis as the owner and manager of the firm. He finally told Dennis that he'd leave if he did not get a pay raise. Dennis told him that was alright with him. The next morning, we discovered missing drawings and the drive."

"Did he share anything about his family?" Sam asks.

"Not much. He became an American citizen twelve years ago, immigrating here from India."

Wanda hollers, "Sam and Kacky, Norman Abrams is here." Norman takes to the stairs and meets Sam and Kacky halfway down.

"Hi, Kacky," Norman says and then reaches to shake Sam's hand. "It's good to meet you in person, Sam. Thanks for the phone call. Please call me Norman."

"Come on up," Sam tells him.

"Sam, I can't imagine living in a log cabin without electricity. How do you do it?"

"Have you ever vacationed staying in a tent for a week or more to escape societal noise?" Sam asks. "It's a bit like that. But you probably still had your cellphone, a laptop with internet, nearby restrooms, water, and the campground-supplied electrical connections. My cabin does not have any of that. It is rustic, and it took a while to get accustomed to it. So, tell me about this newcomer flat you hired us to design."

"As the name indicates, it's an apartment complex for those moving here until they find a home. I thought a simple design could've been completed weeks ago. Headquarters want me to use the same design as what we did in New York and Boston. Sorry about that."

Kacky says, "Are we fired?"

"Norman," Sam says. "You know Dennis is in the hospital with a bad case of the flu and possibly pneumonia. That's what caused the time delay. And the other designer just left and stole some of our drawings. We've recovered all those as they were also saved to a computer cloud drive, that we forgot about. We have it all now. I'm here to finalize it. They'd be ready by the end of the week for contractors to start next Monday."

"Are you sure?"

"Yes. I promise we'll do it, come hell or high water."

"Okay, I'll let headquarters know. We've been granted permission from the city to proceed. I always prefer a local company over a national."

"Thanks, Norman. The contractor will have it in time. Kacky, who are we using?"

Kacky tells Sam the same as we've always used, "Norman Smithian."

"Great. Norman, This other Norman we use is a great contractor, doesn't waste time, and usually finishes a few days or weeks before the expected opening. Is there anything else you'd like to discuss?"

"I heard about you and what a great architect you were. It still baffles me why you'd leave and give all this up for nothing. Oh, I didn't mean it like it came out. Nothing compared to our life here with everything . . . " Sam's phone rings.

"Excuse me. It's my wife. Fran, I'm in a meeting. I'll call you when finished." He hangs up. "Sorry! Back to your question Norman. You said life here with everything. I thought I had everything until I moved there and found more of what I was missing here, which seemed like everything. My favorite place is sitting by a small stream feeding the lake, where I see the birds flying and squirrels running here and there, stopping when they smell a buried nut. I was enthralled seeing an eagle circling the lake and then zooming down to get a fish. Beyond the lake, the forest rose to snowcapped mountains. I would spend perhaps hours there. If all this was by evolution, do you think we'd have a brain that imagines and creates cars, skyscrapers, and computers? All this was created by that magnificent inventor creator God for our benefit, who's watching, loving us in that spirit realm. Because of our continual evilness, He sent His son, Jesus to save us from eternal damnation. Do you know Him, Norman?"

"Sam, it's been great, but I need to go and call headquarters." Norman quickly turns and hurries down the stairs.

Kacky then tells Sam, "that was great."

Sam calls Fran. "Hey, how are things there?"

"That's what I was wondering," Fran replies. Oh, Sam, it's so much fun to watch King in the backyard barking like crazy at the deers and Meredith throwing the ball for him to return it. How's the design coming? Is Dennis getting better?"

"Fran, I'll call later this evening. We've got a ton of work to do. Miss you."

"I miss you, too," Fran replies, and they end the call.

In a few minutes, Kacky brings up the prints of the five drawings and spreads them out on the drafting tables.

"I like 'em," Sam declares after scanning the floor plans. Focused on the outside view, Sam picks up a pencil and starts freehand sketching a different frontal view as Kacky looks over Sam's shoulder.

"Yes, I like it. Wonderful." Kacky says.

Five hours later, Sam says, "Let's take a break. Wanda has a room for me in her home, so I must follow her, unload the car, and have dinner with her and her husband. Then I'll return to the office about seven for a few more hours. You can if you want, or take the evening off. You deserve it. Norman said it must be large enough to accommodate about one thousand. The floor plans you've completed will do that, so take the night off, and I'll see you in the morning."

"Thanks, Sam."

Sam returns later and reviews the plans.

The foundation is good and enough for a contractor to get a start. Four stories high with studios, one-bedroom, and two-bedroom apartments. The first floor has a kitchen, dining room, offices, maintenance area, storage lockers, a gymnasium, and everywhere it's handicap assessable, with three elevators. It's U-shape with a playground between the two side extensions. We need to finish the interior plumbing and electrical system, including the fire alarms.

"Okay," Sam tells himself and leaves the building. On the way to Wanda's home, he calls Fran.

"Hi, Sam. How's it going?"

"Very well. Dennis and Kacky have done a great job. All we need to do is finish the interior plumbing and electrical system."

Fran tells him, "I'll be leaving here on Saturday morning. They've given me a week earlier for my vacation, so be on your good behavior until then."

"Oh. You're spoiling my fun times."

"I will show you what a fun time is when I get there."

"Keep me posted. I miss you. But guess what? Being here and immersed in this, I'm not missing the cabin. Everything is so much easier. Flip a switch on the wall to keep warm, turn on lights, don't have to pump water, stoke the fireplace and stove. I imagine getting out of bed in the morning will be warm and comfy."

"Yes! The same here. You're not thinking of staying there, are you?"

"Fran, I've arrived at Wanda's. Call me later."

***

Two hours later, Fran calls. "Say, hon, I just talked with Susan, and she's excited to see us and meet you too, and the extra week will work more in their favor. How's the plans working? Will you finish on time? How's Dennis? And, what's this with . . . ah, what's his name that suddenly left?

"Paul Adoman. Did you tell Susan where my firm is located? She and Mark could come by sometime. Or, I could go and meet them. Where do they live?"

"In Indianapolis on eighth street, next to the country club. I've got a two-day drive. Leaving Saturday morning. I hope to arrive late Sunday. Okay?"

"Super. Can't wait to see you," Sam replies and hangs up.

Starting early Monday morning, Sam and Kacky work on finishing the plans to submit to the city for approval. Thursday late afternoon, Sam gets a call from the city development office telling him to go ahead. "It's all been approved except for one hitch. Move it back twenty feet further away from the street. The guy from New York agreed that'd be easy.

"Great!" Sam replies. "Thank you. We'll have Mr. Smithian on the site tomorrow sometime, including Norman Abrams from New York, when we can all visualize it on the two-acre site. Perhaps you'll approve the initial digging for Friday?"

"All right, Sam. See you then. And it's nice to have you back in town again."

The city mayor and other city officials, along with Sam, Kacky, and Norman Abrams, opened the groundbreaking ceremony on Saturday at noon. After the mayor cut the ribbon, Norman Smithian, on the back-hoe, made the first dig into the land, and fireworks spread the news.

***

Mark had arraigned a time on Sunday afternoon for Sam and him to tee off.

"Mark, I've only played once since I left here, so excuse me when I start laughing at my horrible shots."

On the fifteenth hole, Sam gets a call from Fran. "I'm here, safe and sound. I'm at Susan's."

"Give us about an hour. I'm having fun letting Mark beat me. And he wants to play again tomorrow."

On the second day with her friend Susan, Fran excuses herself to visit the cemetery where her first husband, Jerome, was buried. Sitting there next to Sam, she relates the fantastic photographic work he did overseas for national magazines. Sam tells Fran more about Angelia, her work as a secretary, and how her sudden death sent him into drunkenness. After that, Fran visited the hospital staff, where she finalized her doctor apprenticeship. Some of those memories are renewed with tears, some with delight.

Sam tells Fran about a few RV vacations he and Angelia took to remote campgrounds. "Getting away from city life for a week or two was wonderful. We loved it and met other couples from other states doing the same. To get away from the noisy city life, fish a bit, swim, take walks through the woods, cook over an open fire, roast marshmallows, and stare out into the wonders of nature."

"Yes, Jerome and I had done that, although we didn't have an RV. We used a tent. We couldn't go far away from home as he was usually on call, and I could've been called in for an emergency. One year, we did make a getaway to Niagra Falls and into the northern woods of Maine. Meredith was eight or nine at the time and missed her friends, but found other girls to run around with, smelling the roses and playing hopscotch. It was mid-fall when the leaves of those trees were falling. I loved to stand under an oak and catch the leaves before they hit the ground. Those were wonderful times. Then he was sent to Iraq, and that was it."

"Yes," Sam says. "Now, here we are. What comes next? I pray that we spend the rest of our lives together. Oh, wouldn't it be great if we both passed on to heaven on the same day, same hour, same minute."

"Fran replies, "are you wishing we'd be killed in an accident?"

"No, no, no. Okay, forget that thought. I was just thinking of the remorse, the sadness I'd experience by losing you."

Fran squeezes his hand. "Yes, me too. But that's out of our control."

A week later, the construction is proceeding very well. Dennis seems to think he'll be back to work next week. After a wonderful meal, Sam, Fran, Mark, and Susan sit on the porch overlooking the golf course. Susan asks Fran if she'd do it again.

Fran replies, "Yes, of course I would. I'm still practicing medicine. The small-town atmosphere is great. The local folks are friendly and positive. Everyone seems to know everybody. Yes, I would do it again." She pauses and adds, "Plus, I met Sam. So here we are, ready to go back home. It's just the extremes we live under in that ancient cabin, but I go back into society every morning for my job."

"How about you, Sam?" Susan says. "I saw it in your eyes that you greatly missed designing homes and all. That museum you created was fantastic. The locals love it, enticing many from out of state to visit, and businesses benefit. You've got that ability, and I'm sure you miss using that gift to design homes for ordinary people. Have you been thinking of staying here? Mark said you indicated how much you miss it."

"Sam, you're not thinking of staying here, are you?" Fran questions.

Sam answers, "Yes, I've had those thoughts at times. Those thoughts have occupied me while here. Becoming an architect was my dream from the sixth or seventh grade. Yes, I've thought of staying and using the cabin for vacations. We've discussed the subject several times when the harshness of cabin life confronts us. Here, you don't even think about where your electrical power comes from. There, our warmth and comfort come from my work. I was offered solar panels or wind turbines, but I refused that. My grandparents lived without all that for their entire life. They cut down trees to create a garden area to grow vegetables to eat and can for the winter months. And, of course, there's fish to catch and eat. One of the difficult things to learn is cooking over a wood-fired stove, which also warms the cabin.

"Susan, imagine waking up in the morning to a coldness because the wood in the fireplace is just ashes. Oh, if I could only train King to add wood to the fireplace during the night. Yes, at times, I wanted to quit or get a nice warm room in a hotel. I arrived in spring, so this was my first winter under those cold conditions. By the grace of God, I managed.

"Am I returning to that cabin lifestyle, or will I stay here and continue with my architectural skills?"

Fran asks, "A simple answer, Sam, please. Yes or no."

"Are you staying here with your friends?" Sam asks.

"Sam, are you going or staying?"

"Will you follow my choice?"

"Dag gone it, Sam. Stop this and make up your mind, so I can make up my mind."

Sam quickly replies, "Oh, You're waiting for me. Mark and Susan, how about that? She's waiting on me. Ok, flip a coin. Heads or tails?"

Fran pokes Sam in the belly, saying, "I'll flip you one, and it'll land on it's end, standing tall."

"Oh, that I gotta see."

'You'll see it all right after it bounces off your nose."

"Go ahead. You've got three tries." Sams pauses a few seconds. "Oh, you're out. Yeah. Out. You struct out."

Susan and Mark look at each other in wonderment.

"You've just witnessed what we do at times," Fran says. "Sam calls it wordy. He starts it when replying to something I said. Catching on may take me a minute. The first time, I thought he had gone off his rocker, and I asked him that, and he replied, no, I'm sitting on my rocker. How can you see me off my rocker. I've realized that we get to understand more of how we think. Anyway, We've got two days to Easter, and then we head back Monday morning. Right, Sam?"

"Yep, Monday morning. I was thinking we'd head up to Chicago to watch the Cubs beat the Colts."

"No, Susan, we're not going through Chicago. Sam, dear, the Colts play football, not baseball."

"I know that. Just checking you out."

"I'll check you out," Fran quickly replies. She breathes deeply and tells Sam it's time to get serious. Mark and Susan, Is Monday morning okay with you?"

Susan replies after noticing Mark nodding his head. "Sure. My schedule Monday morning starts at ten. And, after his retirement last year, Mark has no schedule except for golf."

"You played a good round, Mark. Just four over."

"Thanks, Sam. I could tell by your swing you must have been playing quite a bit previously."

"Yes, I did. I still have some work, possibly a few hours on Saturday morning tomorrow. Easter is clear."

"You've got a beautiful office," Mark says. "I loved the view from the street. The columns set the building off from your neighbors. Susan has already scheduled our vacation for the end of June, so if it's okay with you, we'll stop there for a few days before heading west to Seattle."

"That'll be great," Fran says.

Sunday comes, and after church, the four of them are in a local steak restaurant reviewing their lives in Indianapolis with each other.

Fran interjects, "Yes, Sam, I'm slowly adjusting to the rigors of cabin life. The more I get into it, the more I want to learn. Sam has often said that his grandparents did it for ninety-some years, so he will do it too. And he has. One day at a time, dear Lord.

"Sam likes to bring up history when there was none whatsoever of electricity and thermostats to control the airflow throughout the house. Lincoln did it. Washington did it, and think of the ancients two thousand years ago like St. Paul walking or riding a camel or horse on his long trips to spread the gospel. And what do we do? Not even reach out to neighbors down the block except for a 'Hi there.'

Susan then adds, "In a way, I envy you. It sounds so idyllic, and yes, romantic too. Picturing the two of you in front of the fireplace to keep warm. I would like that."

"When you visit us in June, you'll get that chance," Sam says.

THE
END

Books previously published by Arnold Kropp.

Nov 27, 2012

Mark is a farmer and inventor living the good life with his wife Susan of 33 years. While building up the interest in their Halloween Festival on the farm, Mark gets disenchanted, then obsessed, and desires to leave all the comforts behind to follow a desire for freedom. After experiencing a peace that passes understanding, an unsuspected surprise disturbs their tranquility, forcing them to form new plans.

December 3, 2013

Thoroughly enjoying the solitude of island life for six months, they are suddenly surprised as an old friend shows up with an additional 300 like-minded Americans. The extra people put demands upon them to organize and form a community. This sequel begins as the daily life of building a community continues as surprises from the mainland put them off guard. They are visited by the UN, shocked by Navy jets, and surprised as a small group of Russians locate on the island's far side. All they desired to do was to live peacefully, enjoying the close relationships of family and friends.

March 6, 2020

Yes, I did drive a school bus, and researched it all to provide copies to the other drivers and aides. The school bus. When did it start, how it has evolved, and why? See many pictures of the buses used to transport kiddies to school.

Dec 2014

Just a Matter of Time is a Christian-based novel about a rural family dealing with governmental intrusions brought on by technological advances in every area of life. What will the computerized world of technology be like in ten, twenty, or thirty years? Follow this family of four dealing with the future over four months.

December 2022

Discover who these folks are, what they did, where they went, and where they came from. Yes, we have patios, balconies, apartment service, a banquet-style dining hall, a full kitchen with chef and waiters, our personal mail-boxes, an atrium with a piano and TV. We've got two elevators or stairs to use, an area with a pool table, poker table, and tables for chess or puzzles, a fitness room, *a* barber shop, laundry rooms, a Chapel, a group game room, a TV room, and a library. You can throw horseshoes outdoors, enjoy the walking path. But NO swimming pool or putt-putt golf. Ah, Shucks!

Log Cabin Escape   November 2020

Samuel assumed he was a Christian. A personal tragedy turns his life upside down. He accepts the offer from his late grandfather. He sells his business and home to escape memories. He works at adjusting to life in an old log cabin surrounded by a national forest. A federal agency wants the cabin as a museum. He writes of the insights revealed. He meets the Sheriff. He begins inviting locals out for campfire chats. Boy Scouts enjoy weekend camping outs. A widow gets his attention. The high school principal turns down a request. A class of students comes to see the cabin.

The Sequel to Log Cabin Escape   February 2022

Samuel continues his life in his grandfather's old cabin. He now enjoys sharing this new faith with anyone and everyone. His dog has kept him focused. He get's concerned about invasion threats over his cabin. When a woman doctor administered emergency medical help, he gets the desire for another companion. A journalist visits desiring to capture Samuel's life in an old log cabin. He's forced to change plans for Thanksgiving. But, oh, what a New Year's celebration.